CW01394780

INVISIBLE AFRICA

*Contributions
to a
Coming Culture*

Edited by Ralph Shepherd

NOVALIS PRESS

CAPE TOWN

INVISIBLE AFRICA —
Contributions to a Coming Culture.

Edited by Ralph Shepherd

Copyright ©1996 Novalis Press, Cape Town.

All rights reserved.

No part of this publication may be reproduced,
stored in a retrieval system or transmitted, in any
form or by any means, electronic, mechanical,
photocopying, recording or otherwise, without the
written permission of the publisher.

Published by Novalis Press, P.O. Box 53090,
Kenilworth 7745, Republic of South Africa.

Typeset in 10.5pt Times Roman by
Prototype Graphics and Documents, Cape Town.

Printed in the Republic of South Africa
by Falcon Press, Lansdowne 7780, Cape Town.

Published as a proof edition 1987
Revised edition 1996.

ISBN   0 9583885 7 1

CONTENTS

Acknowledgement   v

Notes on the Contributors   vi

Introduction :   *Stanford Maher*   1

1   **Figures on a Cave Wall**   7
     Johanna Helena de Villiers

2   **The Quest for Equity —**   21
     A Pot of What at the End of the Rainbow?
     Peter King

3   **Spiritual Impulses in South Africa's History**   37
     Hymen W.J. Picard

4   **Lalibela : An Expression of Prester John?**   53
     Rachael Shepherd

5   **Prester John and the Voyages of Discovery**   63
     Ralph Shepherd

6   **The Eastern King**   77
     Evelyn Francis Capel

7   Francisco D'Almeida and   87
    The Cape Of Africa
        Rachael Shepherd

8   Africa, The Heart of the World   105
        J. Lawrence V. Adler

9   Ubuntu in Africa   139
        Mfuniselwa John Bhengu

10 The Servant Leader, a Peaceful   145
    Alternative for a Continent at War
        Ralph Shepherd

11 Mobilization, Mobocracy or Mobile   165
    Waldorf Education in Post-Apartheid
    South Africa
        Brien Masters

12 Angels, Tribalism and the Coming Culture   179
        Ralph Shepherd

The Von Hardenberg Foundation (Novalis Institute) 197

Acknowledgement and Note

This book is the outcome of the endeavours of many friends who have sought to look behind the scenes of violence and instability in the New South Africa — and for Africa as a whole — also for those impulses and indications that will contribute towards the development of a new culture.

Invisible Africa was produced as a proof edition in 1987. Since then great changes have taken place in the world but particularly South Africa. This book has been totally re-written. Some of the original articles have been dropped from this edition and new ones have been included.

The editor would like to thank all those who have contributed to this book, particularly Stan Maher and Charles Abbott who assisted in the editing, design and production.

— Ralph Shepherd

Notes on the Contributors

Johanna de Villiers : doctor of literature, author and poetess.

Peter King : director of Novalis, scientist and lecturer.

Hymen J Picard : author and historian.

Rachael Shepherd : priest of the Christian Community, lecturer and musician.

Ralph Shepherd : director of Novalis, co-founder of Novalis.

Evelyn F Capel : retired priest of the Christian Community and international lecturer.

Lawrence Adler : director of Camphill Village Hermanus, lecturer, and author.

John Bhengu : author, businessman, Member of Parliament.

Brien Masters : Waldorf lecturer, and author.

Stan Maher : author, journalist and lecturer.

Introduction

Africa at the Threshold

STRIP ASIDE the political correctness of the expedient modern world and you find a ready cynicism about Africa. Darkest Africa, it used to be called, a continent of wild animals and wild people. Today, journalists and economists speak of the marginalisation of Africa, a euphemism for giving up on a continent of some 550 million people.

When one looks at the generation-long learning cycles in Angola and Nigeria, the collapse of Liberia and the carnage of Rwanda-Burundi, Western despair seems almost justified. One has, of course, to set aside the failure of Western imagination and will that led to the horror of Bosnia, in order to make this assessment, but Africa gives plenty of scope for horror of its own. After all, say the sceptics, it's the continent that didn't invent the wheel, which absorbs aid like blotting paper and where change and development are slow in coming.

There's another side to Africa that's equally well known, that of heart warmth, honesty and age-old human values that co-exist with the superficial intellectualism of the West. And beyond that there's

1

yet another Africa — Invisible Africa. It's hard to define, but just as cancer appears first in the psychological sphere before it manifests in the physical, so do more positive potentials.

In *Africa, the Heart of the World*, Lawrence Adler gives the analogy of an architect whose mind is at first filled with a spiritual reality in the shape of the design of a building, while nothing physical as yet exists, but who finds once the house becomes a physical reality, that his mind has been emptied of the spiritual impulse which inspired it.

Adler, whose meditative life is a lifetime old, sees Africa in much the same way. This barren, waterless continent can be conceived as an empty space into which a spiritual impulse can incarnate. A picture of what that impulse might be takes shape in the articles in this volume, as stalactites and stalagmites might form on the roof and floors of the Cango caves, the former descending from a world above, the latter growing out of grounded realities.

The articles, though founded in historical fact and in legend, reach into esoteric spheres and throw long shadows. All of the authors strive to go beyond intellectual abstraction to wrestle with ideals and with concepts of substance. There are at least three interweaving perspectives.

Some, like Lawrence Adler and Evelyn Capel *(The Eastern King)*, see the continent as being at a threshold of tremendous significance in its development, and view Africa as a sleeping giant about to awaken. This perspective views Africa against a much longer time-frame than just the post-industrial world, against which Africa measures poorly. It sees a continent whose forces of vitality, like those of an untested youth, will in the end outlast more mature world citizens, with enormous potential not only untapped but unguessed.

Africa, says Adler, is the heart of the world and is destined to fulfil spiritually a function that can be compared to what the physical heart performs for the physical body. Weaving between centre and periphery through the circulation of the blood, the four-chambered heart revitalises the body. The similarly-structured continent of Africa, split by a rift valley whose outrunners rest on the altar of Cape Town's Table

Mountain, offers the opportunity for spiritual impulses to take shape in the physical emptiness of dry Africa. As was the case with the analogy of the architect, as the spiritual sphere empties, the physical one will be filled.

In *The Eastern King*, Evelyn Capel traces the legends of Prester John, the mythical priest-king whose kingdom inspired the Portuguese voyages of discovery to Africa. Ralph Shepherd probes the figure of Henry the Navigator, the seminal figure whose school of navigation prepared sea captains for the voyages mentioned. Linked to the Knights Templar and the Order of Christ, Henry made the search for this ideal kingdom his life's work.

Rachael Shepherd examines the 'ritual murder' on the shores of Table Bay of Francisco d'Almeida, also of the Order of Christ, who apparently possessed Aristotle's last work and defied his religious order to share it, in a presumptuous modern manner, with whomever he liked. This turns out to be Thomas Mallory who was then inspired to write the Morte d'Arthur. His execution was a punishment for crossing forbidden thresholds.

The articles probe ever deeper. *Lalibela*, a priest-king of Ethiopia, travels to Egypt and brings the wisdom of the Invisible Sun that would one day take on physical form and be a companion to humankind. There are links with India, Arabia and even lost Atlantis. The significance of the renaming of the Cape of Storms as the Cape of Good Hope is examined. The themes of hope out of catastrophe, light out of darkness and love out of violence seem very modern.

An evolving consciousness is traced. In *Figures on a Cave Wall*, Helena de Villiers looks at the ways in which Africa's ancient peoples, the San (Bushmen), Khoikhoi ("Hottentots") and modern blacks and whites have viewed the animals of Africa. She finds evidence of preservation of what in Europe is the past, of stages before the development of clear, conscious thinking. A picture of accelerated development emerges, as if Europe had moved swiftly from the age of Roman rule to the industrial revolution, without a Middle Ages and a Renaissance.

Hymen Picard and Ralph Shepherd probe Holland's connection

3

with Africa and the mystical Rosicrucian movement which saw its task as developing clear conscious thought, acting as bridge builders of their age.

The evolution of consciousness in Africa, as in Europe, moves from communal "group soul" thinking to individuation. A new possibility of community life on a higher level beckons, what the Austrian philosopher Rudolf Steiner described in his social ethic:

> *the healthy social life is found when, in the mirror of each human soul the whole community finds its reflection, and when in the community, the virtue of each one is living.*

But that awareness is a step yet to be taken. Peter King, in *The Quest for Equity*, looks at the pursuit of the three lost ideals of the French Revolution — freedom, equality and brotherhood. Freedom has been the watchword of the United States in its development, freedom in everything. Equality is the new buzz word in South Africa, the southern tip where the forces of Western consciousness have penetrated most strongly, and where apartheid appeared most vividly as a thrombosis of humankind's clogged heart forces.

The imagination, as Einstein indicated, is the sphere of thinking that lies above logical, intellectual thought. In times past, self-conscious spiritual beings beyond the physical were conceived of as leading humankind. Today's human, like the Apostle Thomas, doubts scientifically. But our science is hollow at the core. Our physical bodies, the most reliable evidence of our senses, are composed of cells whose average lifespan is a mere two years. And most of the body is liquid which lasts only two weeks. Such security!

The idea of folk spirits or angelic beings overshadowing a culture can be realistically investigated in Africa, where participants in initiatory dances reach trancelike states in which all the dancers move as one being, their limbs the limbs of a single spirit. Our materialistic science is far from such research, pinning its faith in the atom, which turns out to be as empty at its core as the cells of the body are unenduring.

Human life progresses in seven-year cycles, as intuitive wisdom shows: the change of teeth after the first cycle, puberty during the second one and maturity at age 21. We know these cycles continue throughout life and each brings a threshold to be crossed. The 11-year-old climbing trees and living in a body which is, like Greek art, in perfect balance, has no idea of the hormones about to implode his perfect world.

What cycle is Africa going through and what threshold is it about to reach? How will it affect Europe and what is the debt the latter owes to the former, a debt that predates colonial rule as Eden does the Renaissance?

What burden has Africa carried for the rest of the world which it appears about to give up? And what price will the West pay if it fails to recognise the debt and pick up the bill? Indeed, how does a culture which no longer recognises that the thought in the architect's brain is a spiritual reality, value spiritual concepts as creative impulses of which physical realities are merely the effects?

Perhaps an anonymous quotation holds the key: *remember, we are not human beings having spiritual experiences, but spiritual beings having human experiences.*

An unknown, about-to-be-born Africa beckons. Let us follow....

Stanford Maher

Chapter 1

Figures On A Cave Wall

Johanna Helena de Villiers

THE TOURIST POSTERS present South Africa as a country where elephants, lions and antelope are still to be seen in their natural state in game parks like the Kruger National Park or elsewhere. Not more than a century ago the veld was still overrun with large herds of buck. The haunts of lion, rhinoceros and buffalo are remembered in many a place name, so it is understandable that for foreigners, when the name of South Africa is mentioned, the vital creatures of the wilds often arise before the mind's eye.

Perhaps it might therefore be appropriate to consider how animals have been inwardly seen by the various population groups of Southern Africa, with their widely differing cultures at different periods in history. From the way the San or Bushmen, the Khoikhoi or Hottentots, the Black tribes and the English- and Afrikaans-speaking White people represent animals in their stories or poetry, something can perhaps be deduced about different states of consciousness and points of view following each other in time or existing side by side.

The San

The San people present us with a very ancient form of conscious-ness.   One of South Africa's greatest cultural inheritances is to be found on the rock faces of caves and shelters of overhanging rock, often in mountains and inaccessible places: the rock paintings of the Bushmen.   They belong to that ancient hunting culture which has left its traces in other parts of the world as well.   In Europe there are the well-known cave paintings of Lascaux or Altamira, and in the Sahara the rock paintings of the Tassili Mountains for instance.

With unerring precision and vitality the keen-eyed San hunters present silhouette-pictures of animals in movement, singly or in herds, sometimes with hunters or masked figures. Perhaps they created these images with some magical end in view. Sometimes ritual figures in animal masks are recognisable.   From these long-preserved images some researchers infer that the hunter-gatherers believed in a kind of merging between the spirit of man and animal.   Identifying with the animal in a hypnotic dance imitating his movements, the believer would fall down in a trance, and might see himself rising out of his body in an altered state, winged, part human and part animal (David Lewis-Williams, *Seeing and Believing*).   The San believed that the animals were people "of the Ancient Race" before they assumed their present form.

Erik Holm attemps an interpretation of various well-known rock paintings and engravings in the light of what is known about the mythology of the elusive little hunters, who are now almost a vanished race.   A few are left to this day however, especially in the North-West, although the Angolan civil war and cross-border fighting have dis-rupted their form of life.

Holm starts with a rock engraving in which various types of tracks are interpreted as typifying certain animals as belonging to a "moon" type (with cloven hoof) and some as being of a "sun" type, for instance the lion, or the human being, where fingers or toes "radiate" from the central ball of the foot or hand.   He shows how these repre-sentations could have been a lesson presented to candidates for initiation. It might have been intended to teach the cosmic relationship of the various animal species.

We may take it that the Bushmen never saw animals as literally as we of twentienth century Western extraction do. Theirs is an ancient form of consciousness, aware of the language of the stars and apprehending the vibrations of distant objects. They are not yet so alienated from the world of nature as modern man.

In the Bushmen's marvellous and not yet fully appreciated myths the great god is Mantis — a strange insect often seen here, with great vacant eyes and forelegs held together as though in prayer. In other parts of Africa too, insects have imaged the divine, like the scarab in Egypt or the spider Anansi, in Central Africa.

"The People of the Eland" Patricia Vinnicombe calls the vanished Bushmen of the Drakensberge. They loved to paint the eland on their cave walls — perhaps to evoke the spirit of Mantis, who is not portrayed, but was believed to be present in the midst of the eland herds. A creation legend tells how Mantis created Eland out of the waters. The eland is the biggest of the South African antelope, and in some ways takes the place in San veneration which among the Black people was accorded to the bull or cow. Bantu-speaking tribes who drove the cattle-stealing Bushmen away and now live where in ancient times their haunts were, still remember the hunter-god who could be seen in the midst of a herd of eland.

Khoikhoi

Though the cattle-owning Khoikhoi or Hottentots are related to the San, the animal stories they tell are different. Whereas the Bushmen just vanished into the background before the incoming colonists (black in the North, white in the South), the Khoikhoi assimilated the culture of the Western European newcomers. As shepherds or cowherds they told the most delightful animal stories (in their own picturesque Afrikaans) to the little farm children, who listened entranced. The children heard the stories of the battle between the birds and the four-legged animals, or how the birds chose as their king the smallest bird who had cleverly hidden under the eagle's wing in the test to detect the highest flier — old stories which were also known in Europe, and brought to Africa by Dutch and German forebears.

The hero of the Hottentots' "trickster" stories was Jakkals, Wolf, the dupe. (Nomenclature is deceptive. One has to bear in mind that the South African jakkals corresponds to the European fox, whereas our wolf is a kind of hyena closer to the European conception of jackal or chacal.) Some of the trickster stories are told in much the same way among various black tribes, but with different little trickster heroes; for instance Tortoise among the Venda, little Hare among the Shona or Sotho, etc.

One has the impression that in the stories told by the Hottentot raconteurs three traditions coalesced: their own from Africa, the Western European, and another version of the same stories brought by Cape Malay slaves (also Afrikaans-speaking) from the East — from where the themes will have spread originally to Europe and Africa. Of course one of the Cape's early names was "a Halfway Station to the East." (In this pluriform society, with its many paradoxes and surprises, the combining of different cultures into new harmonies seems to be our task all along.) So the stories *Jakkals en Wolf* to the Afrikaans-speaking group, which comprises white as well as coloured members, people originating from Europe and Asia as well as Africa. The language grouping forms a cultural bond right across racial barriers. The so-called Coloured people, a mid-group between black and white, come from very varied ancestry: Khoikhoi, Malay, Black, White, etc. There is considerable stratification of groups who do not always easily mix with each other socially. Today there are not really any Hottentots left in the Republic, they are merged into this larger grouping of "coloured people" (Afrikaans: *bruin-mense*), and the word Hottentot is taboo, carrying a derogatory tone, although sometimes used jocularly by themselves.

The Bantu-Speaking Peoples

The reaction of the Black people to cultural contact was different again. Living in the most varied stages of adaptation between traditional and Western spheres of life, the black people of the different tribes often still manifest a strong communal consciousness.

Another great cultural heritage of South Africa is the treasure trove of Bantu folk tales.　The same age-old themes are recounted with endless variation in the different tribal languages (Zulu, Xhosa, Swazi, Sotho, Tswana, Tsonga, Venda, etc.).　The bull or cow plays a large role in many of these stories, as also in the culture of the black people, where wealth used to be reckoned in the number of cattle a man possessed and the bride-price paid in cattle for a wife formed a kind of living bond between the families involved.　(The laws pertaining to marriage are quite complex.　Traditional tribal law is still recognised where polygamy is practised, next to Roman-Dutch law.)　The atmosphere of some of the stories seems to take one right back to an ancient period of consciousness.　The hero prince for instance comes back from an initiation experience riding on a great white (or sometimes black) bull, with the sign of the moon on his breast.　Leo Frobenius (in Erythraia) gives a whole complex of such stories, intimately connected to the tradition of the priest-king which the Portuguese found when they came to East Africa.　There for instance the Moonking was buried wrapped in the hide of a black bull with a special white marking, to arise again as the moon in the East, with his wife the Morning Star.　Frobenius regards this as the preservation of a "Chaldean" state of mind.　(In Babylonia also, kings or divinities were often pictured on the back of a bovine animal, and the deeds of the earthly king reflected the movement of the heavenly bodies above.)

One story at least from this complex is still popular in Vendaland, Lesotho, and among the Xhosa: that of the boy with the mark of the moon on his breast.　It is the story of the prince who has been robbed of his birthright by a jealous stepmother and abandoned to die.　Various animals aid him through the stages of his growth: ancestor spirits, the bull in the cattlefold, the crabs underwater in the river.　Finally under the protection of "traders" he is recognised as the true heir by the moon mark which he wears on his breast.

Among the black people's folk-tales there are many stories of birds: the bird which keeps returning every time it is killed, for instance, in order to testify to a murder.　Or the stories of the Great Bird who

11

carries young people away to a spiritual land of the ogres, initiation stories of some kind. The *indwe* or blue crane, the national bird of South Africa, is the bird whose feather only chiefs or heroes might wear among the Nguni. And one wonders whether this is not the very same Sun-bird or Phoenix whom the Egyptians portrayed as a long-legged crane in the water — if the stem *ndwenduwe-nduwa* is indeed derived from the hypothetical Ur-Bantu root *zuwa* for "sun," as seems possible.

The crocodile, totem animal of the royal clan, figures in the heraldic emblem of Lesotho. Stories of the crocodile, with whom an "under-water" period of initiation is spent, seem to take one right back to Egyptian Crocodilopolis where the crocodile was worshipped, or to the fire-breathing crocodile of the Book of Job, whose heart "is as hard as the nether millstone."

Of course the snake appears in many guises, as the great water snake for instance, whose fearless bride helps him to be metamorphosed into a prince, or in the impressive python dance of the Venda for girls who are being initiated into womanhood. There is a belief that some snakes embody the spirits of ancestors, very like early Greek belief. (In many ways here we still have physically present among us what in Europe is considered as the past. Is it that stage in the development of consciousness before conscious thinking and full egohood ignite into being?)

The meaning of the animals in Bantu story and tradition is a vast field of study. The wearing of animal masks in ritual dances has to be taken into account, where the dances often represent the spirits of the dead, working in the sphere of fertility of crops and man.

In part of Malawi there was a special ritual to ensure that the "ancestor souls" in the animals to be hunted would return to the pools or rivers which are the ingress to the spirit land, so that in killing a buck the tribesmen would not be acting against the forefather.

There is much fear of witchcraft among the black people. Of an evil person who bewitches others and causes illness or death, it is said that his spirit leaves his body and goes abroad at night in the shape of a baboon. Perhaps this is a true picture of a certain animality

12

which escapes from the soul to do harm when the body is asleep, where evil wishes are present.

White Africans

Between the oral tradition of myth or folk tale and the written literature there is something of a gap. South Africa has not thus far been granted time of gradual transition from early and tribal lifestyles into a Renaissance, such as Europe experienced during the Middle Ages. Between the warrior's assegai and the devastating missile, the sword of chivalry has not yet had time to be forged. (Where would Europe have been if the Celtic and Germanic tribes had moved within decades of meeting the Romans, into the world of the post-Industrial Revolution and the modern city?)

The question arises: How have the white Northerners coming in from the South reacted to the animals of Africa? What form for instance does the image of man's animal nature take in the imagination of English-speaking South Africans, and of Africa's "white tribe" which combines the essence of the various Western-European nations: Dutch, German, French-Huguenot, Scots, etc. (with a salt and pepper dash of Indian or Malay, from the days when the earliest burghers sometimes married liberated slave women from the East?) One would have to see what the poets say.

Although the country now has eleven official languages as a whole it has two main languages. The new nation which was formed on African soil called themselves and their language — African-born and the youngest of the family of Germanic languages — Afrikaans. Perhaps this was the first group in modern Africa who consciously identified themselves as African. In Afrikaans poetry something which lives in the atmosphere of the country surfaces into consciousness, but in a form belonging to the stage of development at which Western-European man now stands, and Christianised. Afrikaans is the language which expresses something deep in the heart of this country, it has been said, while English is the great link with the outside world.

The subject of animal imagery in Afrikaans and English-South

African poetry also is vast. One would like to expatiate on Wilma Stockenstrom's poem of the eland, where the hunter's arrow and the artist's brush coalesce to become an image of man's reaching out to eternal aims; or on Watermeyer's ballad of the bloodthirsty hunter, where all the animals he has ever harmed converge upon the violator of the nature of retribution: an inner mirror image of his own destructive urges. It is hardly right to leave out the eminent poet and naturalist Eugene Marais – a forerunner – who wrote *The Soul of the White Ant*. But for brevity's sake we will only touch on two of the country's foremost poets, N.P. Van Wyk Louw and Roy Campbell.

In 1942 Van Wyk Louw published a volume of poems called *Gestaltes en Diere* ("Apparitions and Animals"). Here we find his poem *Die Strandjutwolf* (a kind of hyena). The fearsome grey animal, in constant invisible pursuit, grows to nightmare proportions. In this volume too are his sonnets *Drie Diere* ("Three Animals"): lying on his bed, he sees himself surrounded by mirrors and in each mirror-wall a tremendous and awe-inspiring animal is reflected: the Sphinx, the Bull and the Eagle. These are no ordinary animals, but great archetypes welling up in the "shining darkness" of the black mirrors. In *Die Swart Luiperd* ("The Black Leopard") the poet goes through stages of descent into a primal world of animal, plant and mineral. The golden eyes of the black leopard glowing in the dark, lure him into a tropical forest and a descent into a deep well ...

> 'n wêreld het in my verstar:
> plant, dier en mens — in diep swart glas
> waar alles enkeld en ontwar
> maar klein en mateloos glansend was
>
> geen ding is duister, maar hy glans
> of hou sy skittering ingesluit,
> en niks is dood, en alles dans
> en reik na naamlose, dinge uit.

In the depths the poet sees everything very small, precise and crystallised. He experiences light and life even in what seems most dark and petrified, and a reaching out towards ultimate aims. The spectrum of the poet's images is that of colour glowing in profound darkness. He is speaking about some deep inner experience. Perhaps (thinking of the leopard Dante met in a dark wood in the middle of his life) a confrontation with sensual experience and a falling away of all the frontiers of normal everyday life. The animal has led him to a deep unity at the root of all being. W.A.P. Smit of the Utrecht University regarded this poem as one of the highest summits of poetry in the language domain which spans Dutch, Flemish and Afrikaans.

In 1941 Van Wyk Louw published his epic *Raka* (passages which have been presented in eurythmy). The story tells of a black tribe confronted by Raka, the ape-man, who is all animal and does not know speech or thought. The tribe's people are fascinated by him and feel a dark lust and terror growing in themselves. Koki alone, the shining young leader, realises the destruction which awaits them if they give way to the mindless violence which silently enters their thoughts. Then there is no one left to guard the gate. Raka, the dark animal, enters.

Koki and Raka express that polarity of high, light-filled thinking and strong, dark will which we often find in Van Wyk Louw's work. In Raka there is no mediating third force, and we are left with the anguish of defeat.

In a later volume, however, Van Wyk Louw places a retrospective poem which points to the possibility of reconciliation between the conflicting elements, *Beeld van 'n Jeug: Duif en Perd* ("Picture of a Youth: Pigeon and Horse"). The bright doves and the dark stallion picture once more the polarity of high, light-filled spirituality and strong, natural vitality. A resolution of the opposition between the light and darkness, "Thought" and "Will," is found through the force of sacrifice, which results in a disciplined control of the dark energies.

The poem portrays an adolescent boy where he sits in a village back yard on a sunny afternoon, doing his homework, and shows him implacably faced with choice. He reads about Caesar's armies — imagines them marching down the white road by the koppie. As the doves circle and peck, and the black stallion snorts in the stable, he remembers also the armies of Cortez in America, and the Aztec sacrifice to the sun. In the sand he traces the emblems of Roman sword, Aztec arrow and Christian cross. He thinks of all the sacrifices that have led up to the death of Christ, until he sees Christ as the unifying meaning of all earth existence:

> ... three crosses above a landscape going dun,
> and, at long last, a free death — and this suspicion:
> perhaps that was able to darken that sun
>
> without an eclipse behind a moon of stone
> because the earth and each terrestrial action,
> the sun itself, even the farthest star
> together simply form a great and single diction
>
> concerning Him and us, is part of His Name ...
>
> — *(Guy Butler's translation.)*

The boy draws a circle surrounded by a triangle. Then he helps Barend, the servant, to catch the beautiful free-running horse, which has been left out to drink. And they shut him in the stable: that wonderful power is under control.

Van Wyk Louw was very reticent about his later development towards a more free and universal Christianity. He died in his sleep, and his last writing, found beside his bed, ended in a prayer. "Even my praying comes from You," he says. "Without that I would just have pushed forward like a pig."

Roy Campbell has a different personality, usually less introspective and more dramatic. Of Celtic extraction, born and reared around Durban in Natal, he left South Africa as a young man and spent most of his later life in Provence, Spain and Portugal, as a bull-fighter, horsetrainer, fisherman, soldier and farmer. He presents himself as a cattle-man and "a son of Abel."

Campbell became known at the age of twenty-two when his long poem, *The Flaming Terrapin,* was published, a poem full of vitality, exuberance and light. The subject is Noah's Ark, drawn through the fearful storm to dry land and a new birth of creation, by an enormous divine Tortoise, who is

> ... the sudden strength that catches up men's souls
> And rears them up like giants in the sky ...
> Built of strong metals molten from the black
> roots of inmost earth ...

> ... the winds and currents
> are his primal thoughts: the raging torrents
> are moods of his ...

> As he rolled by all evil things grew dim.

The great mountain landscape in which after the deluge Noah stands, and finally Man, is for Campbell that of the Drakensberge in Natal.

In some ways *The Flaming Terrapin* prefigures the series *Mithraic Emblems*, published when the poet was in his early thirties. There we find again the vital upsurge of light out of darkness, life out of death, a Phoenix-like rebirth, for

> ... fire is in the Raven's nest
> and resurrection in the tomb.

Mithras is the sun-god of a pre-Christian mystery religion, who overcomes the "bull" of earth and earthly nature. For his followers the flesh of the bull became a sacramental meal, pre-figuring the Eucharist. As someone connected with bullfighting, continuing an ancient tradition, the poet identifies himself with Mithras, "God's cowboy." Perhaps at the back of his mind he also remembered the bull-sacrifices which still take place in KwaZulu/Natal.

> The sun is enemy of my inward night
> and victor of its bestial signs
> whose arm against the Bull designs
> the red veronicas of light ...

There is a wonderful interplay of images and light effects as morning breaks in terms of the songs of the Carmelite St. John of the Cross, the great Spanish poet-mystic whose poems Campbell translated so well.

In Toledo, where John of the Cross had been imprisoned and had begun to write poetry, Roy Campbell became intimately connected with the Carmelite monks, whose lives he saved at the time of the Civil War. The city from which the Star-gazer came who taught Kyot and Wolfram about the Grail mystery, also taught the poet from South Africa about the mystery of the transformation of man's animal nature into a higher state. The culminating poem of the series is an Easter poem *To the Sun* in which Christ himself is

> He who took the toss
> on the black horns of the cross
> and rose snow-silver from the dead.

So we see that in the minds of two of South Africa's foremost modern poets the image of the animal comes strongly to the fore. I suppose they reflect the situation around them. *Mithraic Emblems* comes from the period of the Civil War in Spain. *Gestaltes en Diere* and *Raka* originated during the Second World War. Also great forces of animal violence and frustration build up in Africa where tribal, group-soul people try to adjust to individualistic and materialist Western culture.

In the more Apollonian poet the dark strength is finally controlled, in the more Dionysian the animal dies and is reborn in the light. For Van Wyk Louw light shines out of the dark stone. Roy Campbell sees a rainbow.

The question before South Africa is perhaps: can the instinctive energies of people who are catapulted by the forces of history from a group soul state into technocratic city life — can these animal energies be transformed and controlled to serve the aims of the spirit, or must they dissolve into chaos and violence? In this crisis of transition in the black people's destiny, what insight have their lighter-skinned brothers to offer? It becomes a crisis of development for both. The more intuitive insights of the Black people can conversely also help their White counterparts to grow beyond one-sided intellectuality.

May the beautiful Blue Crane show the way through hard times of adjustment and transition to true inner unity, and Raluvhimba the Eagle who carries the sun through the night to the place where it rises again.

Chapter 2

The Quest for Equity

A Pot of What at the End of the Rainbow?

Peter King

IN THE MEDIA they called it the South African miracle, the birth of a Rainbow Nation.

The steps in the process of transition happened so quickly, and were so incontrovertible, that one hardly noticed the size of their strides and the extent of the changes they invoked. Suddenly the old order was gone, like water through gaps in the floor-boards, and the New South Africa emerged. One wondered where it had been hiding for so long. Perhaps more was incarcerated on Robben Island than just political prisoners.

Undoubtedly it was their release which heralded the series of unprecedented events that followed — the systematic erasure of apartheid legislation; the return of thousands of exiled 'revolutionaries' of the Communist Party, the African National and the Pan African Congresses; the acquisition by the ANC of the prestigious Shell Centre in Johannesburg from which to conduct the campaign that led, with convincing inevitability, to a nation-wide democratic election and, in that instant, a whole new foundation for the country, and a new vista of opportunity. The culmination brought, without doubt, a threshold situation, in the sense that a prospect of great potential was at hand — potential for either harmony or chaos. A threshold ...

It wasn't only in South Africa that this sort of thing was happening. In Europe and Asia during the same period, equally inconceivable events occurred with a suddenness that on a world scale eclipsed those in this country. The Wall came down. New words appeared in the international vocabulary: glasnost, perestroika, reconciliation. The Warsaw Pact disbanded and NATO retired; negotiations which for forty years had tried to establish peace in a cold war were suddenly no longer necessary.

Not only Germany and Eastern Europe, but also the Estonias, Uzbekestans and the Balkans found themselves, like South Africa, in a situation of incipient release from long-imposed constraint — a threat or a threshold depending on whether one's standpoint was in the old order or the new.

Is it far-fetched to look for a common force behind these events? Here we talk about the New South Africa. The Americans speak of a New World Order. There is a sense that something new is necessary in world affairs.

National symptoms reflect an international condition. South Africa, in spite of — some would say because of — its comparative isolation, is representative of the forces at work in our time as much if not more than any other part of the world organism. We are all to some degree, participants. The focus just seems to be that much sharper here.

So, on looking back, what can we make of these events? How do we find our bearings in grappling with the outcomes of new freedom? Will we find a secure point of balance? More importantly what, if anything, can one do as an individual to serve the opportunities that are offered?

Such questions enjoin us to seek a non-political dimension behind the winds of change if we are to find answers of any significance. There is an historical approach which illustrates this.

The starting point is a moment some two hundred years ago. The French Revolution had achieved its immediate aim of demolishing the old order, the old aristocratic regime. And just as it recently happened here, the then people of France suddenly found themselves released, poised on a threshold and faced with a wide open situation.

In Paris, at that critical moment, there appeared a letter from L'Abbe Raynal, pseudonym for the Count of Saint Germain, to the leaders of the revolution.[1] (It would take us too far afield to explore the connection of St. Germain with the Rosicrucian Order. Though not crucial to the historical theme the fact is not insignificant.) In the letter, L'Abbe formulated for the first time the three great spiritual impulses of Liberté, Egalité, Fraternité, giving direction and content to a new order in France. But although they were adopted as slogans, they were not understood. Shortly afterwards the Terror began, followed by the rise of Napoleonism and social tensions in Europe throughout the 19th Century, culminating in the Great War of 1914–1918. In its meaningless horror this catastrophe became the 'War to End Wars', and ironically 'The Last War.' To those who sought meaning in history it was probably the greatest retribution ever inflicted by humanity upon itself.

In 1919, when the Treaty of Versailles was to mark the end of hostilities, and above all to seal the peace for all time, the three great impulses were brought forward again. This time by Rudolf Steiner; but no longer were they mere slogans. He detailed precisely the ways in which Freedom, Equality and Brotherhood can find their reflection in modern society, and gave the admonition that until they are recognised and taken into account no lasting peace can ever possibly come about.[2]

What exactly are these three principles?

The first, FREEDOM, has to do with culture. Culture is not simply an accumulation of artistic expression, as is so often claimed. Culture comprises everything that a country or a people choose for themselves and regard as matters for their personal preference and right to decide. For example, in choice of language, religion, values, customs, medicine, education, ideas, self-expression; in interests, associates and ways of life. Healthy, creative, progressive cultural life depends upon the talents of individuals, diversity of opportunity, and possibility of choice. The operating principle in this realm is the ideal of personal freedom; interference can only stifle cultural development.

But there are also areas of society where freedom cannot be the operating principle. For instance, no-one can be allowed the freedom to choose to drive on the other side of the road. A different principle is necessary. In the realm of law and order and of a person's rights (in this case those of a road-user) the principle is that of EQUALITY, where we all have to do the same thing within certain defined limits, where the individual is obliged to conform. By definition, rights are what we all have in equal measure; having more rights than someone else is privilege. The realm in which equality of rights is the guideline has to do with all these parts of society that are of a political and legal nature: the courts, codes and enforement of law, parliament, policy making and voting. Where equality of rights is operative, participation by any individual is through democratic processes.

There is a third realm in society where neither freedom nor equality are relevant. This is the realm of work i.e. the production, distribution and consumption of goods and services to satisfy human needs. It has to do with the economy and with finance. It is obvious that farmers, manufacturers, builders and traders, for instance, have respectively to comply with the laws of the seasons, laws of efficiency, laws of strengths of materials and of supply and demand. These laws are neither man-made and democratic, nor are they a matter of free choice. They are, so to speak, God-given and inescapable. The greater the awareness of them, and the more skillfully expertise is applied in complying with them, the more successful will be the business.

But skills are not equal in the world of work and many different contributions are necessary: bricklayers, carpenters, electricians — in building a house architects, bankers, foresters, miners, drivers, ad infinitum, are also needed. All the different skills are interdependent. Without collaboration and co-operation, economic life cannot be successful, and, in consequence, some of the people it is intended to serve will suffer. This was summed up in the third principle — BROTHERHOOD. (There is not, unfortunately, a genderless word for this.)

The point that Steiner was making is that just as in an egg we can distinguish the shell, the white and the yoke, so also in any society we can recognise a three-fold structure — first the cultural life and its freedom of individual creativity and development; second, the politico-legal sphere of equal rights; and thirdly, economic activity on the basis of brotherhood. The distinction is not as simple as with an egg. In society the three are intermingled and complex, but they are nevertheless there. Are they perhaps only an Utopian dream?

No one disputes the importance of freedom, equality and co-operation as fundamental aims in human affairs. They are universally accepted and acclaimed as ideals.

Yet when we look throughout the world for evidence of successful triune operation of these three impulses at the present time, we look almost in vain. Why is this? One can ask: what has actually happened to these three principles?

To answer this we have to begin by again going back some 200 years to the connection between the French Revolution and America. This connection was not only in the fact that taxes raised in France to support the American War of Independence were a major cause of the revolution. More important for our present enquiry was the creation of a constitution of the new America, the New World, at a time when the Old World was being racked by the Napoleonic aftermath of the French Revolution. And out of that debris the writers of the American Bill of Rights took the first of the three slogans — liberty — and adopted it as their ideal, their keystone. Freedom of speech, freedom of association, of religion, of the individual. Freedom in political and legal life; freedom in business and industry; freedom in ... you name it.

No matter that a good part of the New World population were dispossessed or slaves at the time, America was to become the Land of the Free. Freedom was established in a way that had never been done previously.

In recognition of this in the middle of the 19th Century the people of France sent an enormous bronze figure across the Atlantic as a gift to the people of America, and erected it in the harbour of New York — the Statue of Liberty. The torch of freedom had been lit. In its dominance it was almost a conflagration.

It was not until the middle of the 20th Century that the second principle began to get firmly established. Equality, as Steiner indicated, expresses itself in the area of rights, legal and political parity. And it was in this area that the demands for universal suffrage, the civil rights concept of Martin Luther King, the abolition of racial and sexual discrimination, independence from colonial rule and so on, manifested themselves, epitomised in the Universal Declaration of Human Rights and the like. People became 'equality conscious', especially in Europe and Africa, just as they had become freedom conscious in America a century earlier.

And just as had happened with freedom, equality and rights spilled over into areas where they did not belong. Demands for equity in the cultural sphere by the radical extremes of women's lib, drop-out cults, gay rights and other minority groups for instance; and political manifestos which talked about 'economic rights' ... in all these the notion of equality becomes a kind of nonsense. But nevertheless, the concept of equality, of rights as the basis of social structure, had irreversibly established a foothold for itself.

The third impulse, that of fraternity — brotherhood, mutual support — we have hardly yet come to grips with. The 'comrade' regime of the old USSR, which obliterated the sphere of personal freedom and reduced equality to a sort of Big-Brotherhood, fell far short of what is needed.

Brotherhood is the operating principal behind the material fabric

26

of society, the production, distribution and consumption of goods, industry and commerce. When Bing Crosby in the depression sang "Buddy can you spare a dime" or when an emergent state now asks the World Bank for millions of IMF units in aid, in both cases the appeal is to the principle of mutual dependence and support — and beyond that to the interdependence of consumer-producer economics. A task of our time is to come to understand what is meant by this, and how to satisfactorily bring it about. The trouble is that trade is world-wide; it is, *par excellence,* a global phenomenon. And it has a life of its own apparently, which we have yet to get to know.

Reviewing the position of these principles of freedom, equality and brotherhood in this way, we have to admit that if one outcome of their harmonious application is Peace, then we are falling a long way short of the ideal, as a glance at any news broadcast from CNN or South African TV will confirm. Nor, taking the analysis of current affairs in the same programmes, does it look as if a complacent hope that we are all slowly moving in the right direction is reasonably justified. Not that TV commentators are necessarily the ultimate arbiters in these things, but their presentations are surely not unindicative straws in the wind. And the straws show that much change is still needed.

A legitimate question therefore arises: what has to happen to mankind — and that means us — if we are to make progress? Let us approach this question at a different angle from the threefold standpoint.

The first thing to take account of is that no outer change can take place in any society without inner change in the people that form it.

For instance, for freedom to be attained in society in any measure, an inner quality of its people is necessary. And that quality, as Steiner pointed out in his "Philosophy of Freedom," is trust.[3] Trust that the other will not abuse his liberty. It is history now, but the first announcement made by the then President F.W. de Klerk after the release of Nelson Mandela was that he felt he could trust him. No other justification was needed.

For there to be equality in civil rights, a different inner quality is

27

needed. The quality which identifies with another person to the ultimate in equality, is that of love. Where love exists, rights can be taken for granted.

When we come to brotherhood the essential aspect is that of mutual support. You may not be your brother's keeper, but you don't let him suffer. It is a question here of responsibility, the counterpoise of freedom.

In short, liberty, equality and brotherhood can exist in society to the extent that trust, love and responsible support live as ideals in individual people.

Now if we consider the inverse of these inner qualities we can get a feel for what they mean, and some idea of the size of the problem. We shall see also that it was not without reason that liberty, equality and fraternity were put in that particular sequence.

Let us first take trust, the necessary pre-requisite for freedom. What is the opposite of trust? If you don't trust someone you doubt him. Doubt runs counter to trust, and the archetypal doubter was Thomas.

Second, take love as the pre-requisite for equality. The opposite of love, in the sense it is used here, is denial. Without love you can deny someone their rights, and this was one of the most fundamental objections to apartheid. But the principle operates on many levels: "Do you love me?" asked Christ repeatedly of Peter. "Of course," came the repeated reply. "Before the cock crows you will deny me thrice." Peter became at that event the archetype of denial.

Third, brotherhood. When you don't give inner support to your brother it is something much deeper. When you let down someone you could have held up, you betray the humanity in him. Betrayal is the opposite of support, and the archetypal betrayer was Judas.

The Bible tells us something further about these three :

When Thomas found himself guilty of doubting he probably felt somewhat ashamed of himself.

After Peter realised he had denied Christ, he wept.

But when Judas became a betrayer he hanged himself.

Do not these give some measure of what is being demanded of us if the three spiritual impulses are to be realised?

If there is any substance in this approach then it is useless to try to organise and expect change "out there" without first bringing about some inner changes. To emphasise a need for shifts in attitude is not moralising; it has a force of practical necessity. And it is obviously not easy.

To attain freedom by cultivating trust, as opposed to doubt, is comparatively straightforward. That one came first, as I have tried to describe. To attain equity in human rights by cultivating love is more difficult, especially when it is other people's rights at issue rather than one's own. That gained a firm foothold during the past fifty years or so. There may be much confusion about what exactly freedom is, as distinct from a right, but both are acknowledged as fundamental and essential components of any social system, which can never be built on doubt and denial.

When we come to the attainment of brotherhood in economic life, however, it is a different story. And I believe it is just here that we come face to face with one of the major tasks of the times we are living in.

It doesn't take much to see that behind most of the discord and uncertainties of the present time lie the still unsolved questions of economics. Questions to do with livelihood, ownership, distribution of wealth, unemployment, monetary policies, marketing, monopolies, exploitation, the purposes to which industrial production is put, the imbalances of benefit and detriment to the planet, etc. The list is long and arguably getting longer. Each item in it is a threat to somebody, and each threat calls up a reaction in the interests of security that threatens someone else's interest. The Gulf War — a war fought ultimately to secure oil, the life blood of industry — was evidence, if evidence is needed, of the ferocity of the forces that are allowed to drive our economic life. That is an extreme example.

One of the fallacies we have inherited from the nineteenth century is the notion that it is competition that makes the world of economics go round. Competition has its place — in the acquisition of under-standing of the given laws that underlie all economic activity, for example, and in the skills to work with them. But a moment's thought shows that consumers do not compete with producers. They depend on one another. Neither could exist without the other. And since we are all both consumers and producers in the world, co-operation must be the fundamental concern; and brotherhood — responsible two-way support — the principle.

There are many other inherited notions, equally misleading — that technology can find answers to social problems; that nature evolved to its perfection through survival of the fittest and mankind can improve its portion in the same way; that there is a capitalistic management class and the workers, etc. We still have a wealth of fallacy in scientific concepts about the nature of our world, born in the last century and now hardened into dogma that constitutes an unspoken faith by which we conduct our affairs. A faith, we could call it materialism for short, that is virtually international in all matters where money is concerned.

Little wonder, then, that the skirmishes fought daily in corporate offices, conference centres, promotion agencies, union meetings, board rooms and the like, where the invisible strings that motivate the strategies of commerce and industry are created, are at bottom not fundamentally different from the self-interest objectives of Desert Storm in the Gulf.

At the end of the 20th Century there is nothing new about ideas such as these, nor about the disillusionment and dissatisfaction with them that get wide condemnation in environmental, holistic, new age and such-like coverage.

In South Africa there is a new term of condemnation that has caught on with some post-apartheid academics — Eurocentricism. To call a thing Eurocentric implies that it is alien, unsuited and inappropriate in an African context. Colonialism, racism, multinational corporations and liberalism fall into this category. So do the 'old' standards and methods in the conduct of business. The fact, however, is that there is hardly anything among the aspirations of the whole nation that does not have its origin in Europe. Water reticulation, plumbing, electricity, jobs, football, Volkswagens, cellphones, democracy, and so on;

these Eurocentric things are as ubiquitous and as sought after as Coca Cola. European or not, everyone wants them. The Eurocentric protest is simply one aspect of the problem of the new South Africa. The problem of identity.

How do you forge a nation from eleven official languages and as many cultures in an industrialised country that is predominantly black, where the major proportion of support of a first-time government is from people living in traditional or make-shift huts? What flag can be nailed to the mast? More importantly, what unifying values can the flag possibly represent?

At the moment of writing this article, the two-year task of creating a new Bill of Rights and Constitution for the country is nearing completion. This is pre-eminently the 'rights realm' in action, and the debating process has been scrupulously democratic. Anyone can chip into the deliberations with strictly equal opportunity. Transparency, participation and negotiation are the buzz words — a far cry from the faith that attended the efforts of the Founding Fathers. There is reasonable expectation that these documents of intention, and the constitutional court that will administer them, will provide a South African anchor of stability for its public and legal affairs.

But voyages are not made at anchor. What is to happen in the cultural realm with its diversity of talent, freedom of choice and free development of personal and professional values? What, on the other hand, is to happen in the realm of economic, industrial, business, financial life of the country?

Some indication of what might happen is shown by what has historically been a characteristic tendency of approach to these three realms in South Africa.

In the West, in America, it was the realm of freedom that dominated. Priorities were given to its corresponding features: individual initiative, free marketing, federal association, control based on competition rather than constraint, often at the expense of the other two realms.

By contrast in the East, under communism, the criteria of production and distribution largely determined the way things were done:

the collective good, co-operative conformity, republican organisation, the normalisation of standards and a culture subservient not to the individual but to the State.

Neither of these extremes occurred in South Africa. Here for the past half century the distortion of extremes has manifested in the middle sphere. Under apartheid the whole of life fell under the sway of government and the statutes it promulgated.

Freedom in cultural and personal life was limited by a race-based doctrine and the standards of a Christian Nationalism embodied in the law. Education was the most telling example.

The economic life did not escape either. As government increasingly infiltrated into industrial and commercial activities through parastatal and most-favoured enterprises, so the economy became hedged with regulations and conditions of employment and production. Government Boards of control, using political criteria, directly through law and indirectly through Broederbond membership, determined the production, infrastructure and distribution of electric power, water, resources, fuels, land development, meat, milk, mealies, eggs, sugar; I'm told there was even a Banana Board. The administration of the system required one of the largest per capita civil service organisations in the world.

The point to be made is not only that the government and its system was not based on democratic equality and therefore inherently unjust, that it enriched whites at the expense of blacks, or that it was cumbersome and impregnable.

The point and tragedy is that two or more generations have now grown up with the conviction that it is only through government that power can be wielded and a country developed.

The mission to expunge apartheid from the land and destroy its system, has obscured the fact that it wasn't only the motives of government that were the abomination. It was also the fact that government used the law to encroach on and control the freedom of individuals and the functions of the economy. Any government that does that is interfering in areas where it does not belong. If there is any truth in the need to recognise the three areas of operation in

32

societies and to respect the distinct and different principles that are appropriate to each, then in the long run such interference, even if it has apparent benevolence, can only result in ultimate stultification or loss of peace, or both.

It is understandable that in its quest for equity the African National Congress should regard its dominant governmental position (in collaboration with the Communist Party, the Congress of Trades Unions, and the National Party in the transitional Government of National Unity) as the essential power base for effecting change and reconstruction in accordance with the perceived rights of the people. In this task it has widespread, informed support.

It is also understandable that the dangers of encroachment and interference, of bringing politics into culture and into economics, are not heeded. Why should they be? South Africa has always been riddled with politics and politicians, it's the way things were always done here. Among other things, under apartheid it got a lot of otherwise unemployable people into jobs. Why change now?

It is perhaps too soon to draw definitive conclusions about the way things will go in the New South Africa. The brooms are new, and there is a lot of sweeping to be done. It would be carping not to acknowledge the enormous amount that is being done and the goodwill, care and responsibility being given to the task.

At the same time, one has to be very starry-eyed not to see some of the warning signs.

Some examples: the civil service, disproportionately large under the old regime is becoming under the new dispensation even larger; and the gravy train, if the media are to be believed, is even longer. There is in addition a proliferation of part-time civil servants on advisory and policy committees with state-paid expense accounts and concessions. These could conceivably self-correct in time, but there are gradually emerging signs of controlling rather than facilitating functions. The Reconstruction and Development Programme, pre-eminently dependent on economic and practical expertise, has been bogged down by centralised planning and democratic red-tape since its inception. Centralisation of power, and control over cultural and

33

economic decision, appears to have become an issue of unsolvable contest with the provinces of KwaZulu Natal and to a lesser extent in the Western Cape.

Education, the professional domain of teachers, looks like becoming as constrained by controls and Governance structures — or it will as soon as the structures start functioning — as it ever was under the old regime, albeit the aim is equity. Some tertiary institutions are still being vandalised and periodically closed down by students demanding the right to enrol irrespective of their previous scholastic attainment or ability to pay fees. Trade unions, as happened elsewhere, have adopted a political role and wield significant power, in the formation of Government policy, and often in matters commercial and industrial decision, on the grounds of the presumed right to jobs by their members. Affirmative action, and so on.

All of these can be, and are, argued on the basis of political expediency and the interests of equity. But that is not the purpose in listing them. All of them seek to solve problems. All of them, in the instances listed, are using political criteria to solve problems that are either cultural or economic. It is not realised that their solution demands consideration of the issues of freedom or of mutual support, not democracy.

In the New South Africa, all has to be democratic. The popular belief is that democracy can't be wrong. The trouble is that in certain areas of decision, where a federal or republican approach would be better, democracy can create more problems — of stultification, frustration and ineffectualness — than it solves. How and why this is so has been the purpose in writing this article.

None of this is to imply that democracy as the means of ensuring political equity and civil rights is not important. South African recent history (and not only South African) has demonstrated again that democracy is essential as the balancing component in social order. But it is only one of three components. The other two are equally essential.

The success so far of the transformation towards a New South Africa stands above all to the credit of Nelson Mandela. It is he alone who has had the prestige, the acumen, the vision, the critical insight and the happy knack of the common touch, to give spiritual steam to the process.

In 1999, the next elections, the replacement of the alliances in the Government of National Unity by the more usual parliamentary governing party and an opposition, and the retirement of Nelson Mandela from the Presidency, will all come to pass. Of these, it is the loss of the leadership of President Mandela that causes most apprehension. Without his guidance and influence, people ask, will the new arrangements survive? There seems no visible personality in public life who could even remotely fill his shoes.

The answer given by Madiba himself rests in the creation of a new nationalism. The inauguration ceremony, the rugby cup, and winning performances by national football and cricket teams were certainly nation building occasions. But a country which already consists of many long-standing nations is unlikely to find cohesion by prowess of some of its citizens in sports. In any case, nationalism has proved itself an uncertain anchor in today's world.

Is it not so that inner stability, strength of purpose and international respect derive above all from the spiritual values that a nation or a people exemplifies?

Three of the greatest impulses of nationhood, not as fully realised as they could be, yet everywhere held as ideals, are the three great principles of freedom, equality and brotherhood.

South Africa is recognised for its quest for equality. Whether all its citizens will also be able to find freedom and brotherhood remains to be seen. If they can, then the country may find peace in the pot at the end of its rainbow.

REFERENCES

1   Rene Querido - Essay *Reading the Signs of the Times*. Published in a booklet "Michael's Struggle with the Dragon". Rudolf Steiner College, Fair Oaks, California, U.S.A.

2   Rudolf Steiner - *The Threefold Social Order*. Anthroposophical
     Society, Dornach, Switzerland.

3   Rudolf Steiner - *The Philosophy of Freedom*. Rudolf Steiner Press,
     London. ISBN 0 85440 090 7.

Chapter 3

Spiritual Impulses in South Africa's History

Hymen W.J. Picard

IN THE COLOURFUL STORY of South Africa's development from a tiny Dutch colony in 1652 to the wealthy Republic of today, in which 43 million black, brown and white people desperately try to mould a political constellation offering a happy future for all, the name of Stellenbosch deserves to be written with capital letters. Although to the more casual observer Johannesburg with its gold, Pretoria with its status as Capital, Durban with its harbour and Cape Town with its scenic beauty and as seat of Parliament, may be better known and appear more important, it is Stellenbosch with its University that contributed most to the building of that remarkable young nation — the Republic of South Africa.

No less than six of the country's eight prime ministers, from 1910 when it became a British Dominion under the name of 'Union of South Africa', to 1983 when the Constitution was changed and an Executive President replaced the Premier, were former students of the University of Stellenbosch, whereas the present State President is the University's chancellor. Political contrasts like General Jan Smuts, international statesman, co-founder of the United Nations and philosopher of the Holistic Doctrine; Dr Daniel Malan, staunch nationalist and orthodox Calvinist; gentle but stubborn Barry Hertzog with his famous slogan "South Africa First!"; aggressive Transvaler Hans Strydom, nick-named Lion Of The North; brilliant professor of ethnology and creator of the policy of Separate Development, Dr Hendrik Verwoerd; and able lawyer John Vorster; they all were trained and mentally shaped in the lecture halls of Stellenbosch's Alma Mater.

Grown out of the 'Stellenbosch Gymnasium' which was founded in 1863, via the 'Stellenbosch College' in 1881 and the 'Victoria College' in 1887, Stellenbosch University acquired its full academic status in 1918.

In virtually all domains of human endeavour, in so far as the shaping of the South African nation is concerned, Stellenbosch-trained men took a leading role. In the field of economics former Stellenbosch students Dr C. van der Byl (Iscor – Iron and Steel Corporation), Dr J. van Eck (Industrial Development Corporation), Drs F. du Toit and P. Rousseau (Sasol – the country's oil from coal plant), and Dr C.R. Louw (Sanlam – the biggest Insurance Company in South Africa) vitally contributed to the country's prosperity and sound reputation as a good region for investment. In the same context it is still today the Bureau for Economic Research of the Stellenbosch University that issues the most authoritative and reliable statements of present and future economic trends and expectations. It is even significant that Dr Anton Rupert (Rembrandt Tobacco corporation) chose Stellen-bosch as the centre and headquarters of his industrial empire, and supervises his factories in the U.S.A., Australia, and other countries from his modest office in Stellenbosch.

In the field of agriculture it is the highly esteemed Elsenburg Agriculture College (since 1918 part of the university) that, through

38

its training of agriculturists, research and information, greatly contributes to the feeding of the country's fast growing population and even more than that: to the feeding of many hungry millions in neighbouring countries!

As the Republic's only university with a five year course in engineering and a faculty of Military Science, Stellenbosch University also assisted in establishing the country's arms industry; and by lending its professors to the Military Academy at Saldanha, is instrumental in the forming of a cadre of officers for army, air force and navy that, according to foreign experts are among the best in the world.

It was at Stellenbosch University that South African students for the first time cheered a black foreign leader: Dr Hastings Banda, President of Malawi. At that university, marxist theoreticians may lecture next to ultra-conservative dominees and Jesuit Priests. It was in the student residences and on the sportsfields of Stellenbosch where the first seeds were planted from which enlightened nationalism could sprout and ripen. It is that enlightened nationalism which produced the Nkomati Accord, the Treaties with Swaziland and Lesotho, and the dramatic political reform programme announced by President P.W. Botha in his opening speech to Parliament in 1987. This enlightened nationalism is also proved by the group of Stellenbosch students who wanted to talk with the African National Congress in Lusaka against the wishes of the then South African Government.

Why is this so? Why could the picturesque little town, situated fifty kilometres from Cape Town, shaded by countless oak trees and embellished by numerous Cape Dutch gables, play such a vital role in the moulding of the Republic of South Africa and in the process of political reforms now in full progress?

To the man in the street — even in South Africa itself — the white history of this country began when Dutch Commander Jan van Riebeeck planted the flag of the United Netherlands Provinces on the shore of Table Bay. It was there and then on 6th April, 1652, that the first white settlement was established at the Cape of Good Hope as a refreshment station for the many Dutch ships and their crews that sailed to the Far East and back. And since the present Republic

39

ultimately grew out of this tiny settlement, one cannot say that the man in the street is altogether wrong. One may even go a step further in supporting his cause. Jan van Riebeeck allowed a few employees of the Dutch East India Company (who ruled the growing colonial empire of the Netherlands) to leave their service and settle as so-called 'freeburghers'; and this little group actually formed the embryo of the present nation.

However, when one is aware of the fact that matter has its origin in spirit, and that historical facts can only be truly understood if one knows their spiritual background, Van Riebeeck's deed of creation is less significant than that carried out by Commander (afterwards Governer) Simon van der Stel in October 1679, when he founded Stellenbosch only a fortnight after his arrival as the new administrator of the Cape Settlement.

The spiritual differences between Van Riebeeck's impulse of founding the Cape Settlement and Van der Stel's impulse of founding Stellenbosch, is that the former was the result of an instruction, a command, given by a commercial body to one of its servants; and the latter the outcome of a vision flashing up in the soul of an individual. The 'Caapse Vlek' (Cape Hamlet) as Cape Town was originally called, came into being because the seventeen directors ("Lords Seventeen") of the Dutch East India Company felt the need for a halfway station to refurbish their ships on the long haul to the Far East. They despatched Jan van Riebeeck to the South Western point of Africa, and as their dutiful employee he obeyed and obliged. Twenty-seven years later Simon van der Stel rode out with his officers to inspect the outlying districts. Suddenly he pulled up, looked around and said: "At this place I want a new settlement."

It is quite immaterial whether apart from the beauty of his surroundings he recognised their agricultural potential. The quintessence of his deed was that he followed the dictates of his own EGO. In fact he acted against the wishes of his superiors in Holland who did not want any new settlements.

To put it more concisely: Cape Town's embryo was conceived by an agent of an outside power that ordered him to do so; Stellenbosch's birth was effected by the intuitive creative urge of a single individual. For that reason I dare state that the founding of Stellenbosch was a cosmic deed in contrast to the founding of Cape Town which was an earthly deed.

When one scrutinizes the life of Simon van der Stel, many indications and even facts are revealed which illustrate the man's spiritual consciousness.

He was born at sea near the island of Mauritius during a howling storm. Dr. Rudolf Steiner told us something about the meaning of such a birth, a birth in fact outside the area of any folk soul in so far as such beings are area-bound. He spoke of people who are spiritually not limited to a certain, small section of the earth. It therefore is clear that Simon van der Stel was innately more open to cosmic influences than people born on land.

As a child of five Simon van der Stel watched the total destruction of his father's settlement on Mauritius by a hurricane. A few years later, on Ceylon, he saw his father's bleeding head carried into a fortress of the Dutch East India Company after Singalese rebels had killed Van der Stel Senior. Soon afterwards young Simon met in Batavia (capital of the Dutch East Indies) with his maternal grandmother, Monica da Costa, a half-caste or possibly even a trueblooded Indian lady, and consequently for a while he was exposed to the radiation of ancient Indian wisdom.

His primary and part of his secondary education Simon received at a school in Batavia but at 19 he was sent to Holland to finish his studies. Sojourning at Van Riebeeck's halfway station at the Cape of Good Hope, the boy witnessed the vandalism of drunken sailors rampaging through the fruit and vegetable gardens which were not just the pride of the young colony, but the purpose of its existence. One may only surmise that it was then and there that Simon van der Stel had his first vision: a new and better garden, laid out and developed by himself. This becomes more than a mere speculation when one learns that the later Cape Commander Van der Stel established a Company garden that, according to French visitors in 1685, favourably compared with their Sun King's great creation at Versailles. And

41

moreover, that this horticultural job was among the very first activities Simon undertook when he returned to the Cape as Commander in 1679.

Whatever happened to the youngster that fortnight at Van Riebeeck's, it is obvious that something was aroused in his soul that kept calling him back through the following twenty years. From the day he arrived in Amsterdam his ambition became clear: everything he undertook points to his desire to return to the Cape of Good Hope as its boss, and to turn the colony into something great and beautiful. Even conventional historians who reject all references to spiritual interferences in earthly events, found it strange that so young a man would devote twenty years of his life to training for a position that was far out of his reach. Simon studied history, geography, mathematics, astronomy, agriculture and viticulture. He worked as a merchant, a farmer, a winegrower and a soldier.

Even his courtship and subsequent marriage may be seen in the light of his unswerving plans for the future. Thanks to the painstaking research done by the South African historian, Dr. Anna Boeseken, for her book *Simon van der Stel en sy Kinders* (Simon van der Stel and his Children) one knows that Simon's married life was far from happy. His wife, proud Johanna Six, was the daughter of one of the most influential merchant families in Amsterdam, and closely related to Johan Bax van Herenthals, Simon's predecessor as Governor of the Cape. Johanna's hand was quite a prize for a penniless orphan from the Dutch East Indies, and when it was his for the taking he did so with alacrity. Although the couple had children, known facts about their wedded life indicate that husband and wife were continuously at loggerheads. Their association came to an end when at last Simon saw his burning ambition fulfilled and went to the Cape as its Commander. He took all his children along, but not their mother. This can only strengthen one's impression that his was a marriage of convenience.

That young Simon van der Stel was indeed obsessed by his urge to return to the Cape as its ruler is also demonstrated by the fact that already long before he could expect to have a fair chance of getting the post, he applied for it, not once but several times. Another indication is that he with his excellent education and many-sided training, his intelligence and willpower, and last but not the least his outstanding connections with Holland's commercial aristocracy, never sought a position in his motherland or at least in the East Indies where sophisticated Batavia attracted many brilliant youngsters. No, Simon aimed at a badly paid job in a rather obscure and tiny settlement with too little civilization and too much wind.

Assessing the influence of Stellenbosch's thinking on the development of the Republic of South Africa in the light of the strange obsession of the town's founder to become administrator of the Cape Colony, I came to the conclusion that there was more to Simon van der Stel than the history books and conventional biographers conveyed.

It was during the research for my biographical novel 'Man of Constantia' that under the guidance of an old acquaintance of the Far East, the unforgettable Max Stibbe, I began to read the works of Rudolf Steiner and became active in the Anthroposophical movement in Cape Town. This meant that the whole tenet of my historical researches and writings changed. For the first time in my long career as journalist and author I became aware that spiritual forces lead world history along certain paths to certain goals. What had lived only vaguely in me before — that the individuality known as Simon van der Stel had something that distinguished him from other Cape Governors — now became clear. My investigations were now directed at such events as ought to have left an impression on my subject's soul life. I tried to discover who his friends had been; in what circles he had moved during his long stay in 17th Century Holland; what his personal interests, his fancies, his hobbies had been. And naturally I discussed my findings with the instigator of my new historical outlook, my friend Max Stibbe. Everything I could tell him about Simon van der Stel led Max to the conviction that this remarkable ruler of the Cape of Good Hope had either been an active Rosicrucian or at least a strong sympathiser.

Perhaps not all our readers know that Holland, or rather the United

43

Provinces of the 17th Century (the so-called Golden Age) had close connections with the Rosicrucian movement as it had grown out of Christian Rozenkreutz's original triumvirate of wise men (afterwards increased to eight) and was spreading its message of a purified Christianity and a union of mind and spirit throughout Western Europe. Although in none of Dr Steiner's lectures confirmation could be found of theologian Prof. Dr. J.B. Semmler's allegation that the child Christian Rozenkreutz was brought up in a monastery near Zwolle, in the Eastern part of the Netherlands (where the famous author of the Imitatio Christi, Thomas a Kempis, was a fellow pupil) and served as assistant to Bishop Floris Radewyns and Geert Groote during their alchemistic experiments, it is well known that the Rosicrucian doctrines gained staunch support among that country's cultural leaders. The Fama and the Chemical Wedding were widely read.

Throughout the centuries the Roman Catholic Church — and since the middle of the 16th Century Calvinism also — had zealously persecuted all who dared attack their teachings. Consequently Rosicrucianism faced great dangers and the 'operations' of the Brotherhood had to be carried out in secret. This is obviously the reason why so little is said in our history books about the profound influence Rosicrucianism had on 17th Century thinking, particularly in the Netherlands, West Germany and England. Even in Holland with its reputation for tolerance — the country where a Descartes could publish his, for that time, revolutionary writings and a Spinoza could print his heretical manuscripts — Rosicrucians and their sympathisers were not able to profess their beliefs openly and even less to admit that they were members of the Brotherhood. When they did so, they paid dearly for their audacity as the well-known painter Torrentius found when he was dragged before a Calvinistic Court in Haarlem and most cruelly tortured. In Amsterdam too, though the centre of spiritual and intellectual freebooting, the Rosicrucian Brotherhood had to tread with the utmost caution. There were no headquarters, no offices or clubs, where Rosicrucians could openly meet. So only the members knew that the famous Rederyckerskamer (a kind of literary and theatrical society) "In Liefde Bloeiende" (Blooming through Love) with

44

a red rose and other symbols in its coat of arms, was a camouflaged meeting place of Rosicrucians. It is important to mention in this context that the painter, Rembrandt, was an active member of that Rederyckerskamer.

This was the Amsterdam where Simon van der Stel studied and later lived with his wife, Johanna Six, niece of the well-known magistrate and art-patron, Jan Six, who was depicted in one of Rembrandt's greatest portraits and who acted for many years as the painter's sponsor. It is therefore not too far-fetched to assume that Simon met Rembrandt and possibly knew him well.

To increase his knowledge of viticulture Simon bought some lands and planted vineyards near Muiderberg Castle. Here the poet Hooft, scientist Huygens and many other cultural VIP's came together in the Muiderkring (Muider Castle) to discuss contemporary trends in philosophy, science and art, and undoubtedly also what we now call spiritual science. Hooft himself had died at the time of Van der Stel's viticultural experiments, but it is known that the meetings of his friends and pupils went on for many years after his death.

It would naturally be over-hasty to deduct from these facts that Simon van der Stel was a Rosicrucian, but seen in the light of other known data of his activities in the Netherlands and afterwards at the Cape, these facts fit tightly in the total Rosicrucian image that could be reconstructed.

According to students of 17th Century Rosicrucianism an interest in chemistry and geology was most significant. From official reports issued in 1685 we know that the then Commander of the Cape Settlement was well versed in the science of Scheikunde. I use the Dutch word for chemistry intentionally because it defines much better than the English what this science originally aimed at. Scheikunde is literally the knowledge of separating, i.e. separation of substance. This science was until the middle of the 17th Century still closely linked with its forerunner — alchemy. And we all know that the practice of alchemy was a must for all contemporary intellectuals who tried to fathom the mysteries of the Cosmos. In fact, the carrying out of alchemical experiments was one of the main duties of the Rosicrucian

Brotherhood.

A second desideratum, closely connected with the first, was to search for minerals and study them. Simon van der Stel's wish, or rather, urge to penetrate into wild and unknown Namaqualand to look for copper, is telling. We know from his letters to his Directors in Holland how strongly he insisted on this scheme. After the attempts of his second-in-command, Olaf Bergh, had been fruitless, Van der Stel himself organised a well-equipped and well-planned expedition which included a boat for crossing the rivers and a couple of musicians to keep up the morale. And indeed, he discovered the green-sloped mountains of Manaqualand and personally melted the ore which produced the first copper processed in South Africa.

Even today Van der Stel's bold venture into the unknown continues to appeal to the imagination of young and old. In October 1986, on the occasion of the expedition's tricentenary, it was reconstructed down to the smallest detail and wherever the horsemen in their 17th Century apparel passed, they were enthusiastically cheered.

Naturally one might suggest that the search for copper could have a purely materialistic motivation — profit. However, as in the case of the founding of the new settlement Stellenbosch, the Lords Seventeen in the Netherlands were not at all keen on this copper initiative of their Cape Commander. Apart from the lack of transport if copper would indeed be found, there was the danger of turning the militarily weak Cape Colony into a treasure house with all the risks emanating from that. But even if Van der Stel's motive for his copper search contained a materialistic element, this would in no way contradict his spiritual urge. Many famous Dutch Rosicrucians combined their awareness of spiritual values with astuteness in the art of trade and industry. It was exactly because Rosicrucians saw it as their task to further the development of consciousness, i.e. of clear and factual thinking, that so many Netherlanders became Rosicrucians.

Perhaps the most striking example of this is Louis de Geer of whom we are just about certain that he was a Rosicrucian. De Geer established an industrial empire of mining, ship building, armaments and other vital requirements for countries that were daily at each other's throats. This forerunner of the present-day industrial tycoon built a complete navy for Sweden and by doing so uplifted this weak and almost bankrupt country to world-power level — for which he was ennobled by the Swedish King. This same materialistic aspect of Rosicrucianism, or rather this most extreme expression of the Consciousness Soul, was projected by Christian Rozenkreutz himself in this 18th Century incarnation, when as the Count of St. Germain he founded — apart from his numerous Rosicrucian lodges — many textile, paint and pottery factories in the Netherlands, Belgium and Austria.

Another command of the Rosicrucian syllabus in the 17th Century ordered the brothers to strengthen not only mankind's three soul forces — thinking, feeling and willing — but also man's surroundings; in other words, to purify and embellish man's environment. This duty was coupled with their healing task which was one of the first instructions Christian Rozenkreutz had given to his pupils. Effective healing is only possible in a clean, unpolluted environment, and therefore the creation of such surroundings was a primary Rosicrucian objective. The importance of this commandment in a time when hygiene was virtually non-existent is self-evident.

If ever an administrator of the Cape, Dutch or afterwards English, looked after the cleanliness of his domain it was Commander (since 1690 Governor) Simon van der Stel. From the day of his arrival in the Settlement in October 1679, he issued a stream of proclamations urging the citizens to keep their little town clean, lay out gardens and plant oak trees. Van der Stel himself planted numerous oaks in and around the Cape Peninsula and Stellenbosch. Apart from embellishing their environment, oak trees supplied valuable timber for ship building and repairs. In this instance again Van der Stel's practical considerations supplemented his spiritual commitment.

The same applied to his planning and building the new hospital at the corner of today's Adderley Street and Wale Street opposite the Old Slave Lodge, which nowadays accommodates the Cultural Historical Museum. In this case the spiritual motivation was in agreement with the Company's wishes because of the importance of curing employees who would otherwise be a financial burden. Be this as it may, Van der Stel proved his very advanced consciousness by creating a hospital that in all its facilities was far ahead of any similar venture outside Europe. It offered beds to five hundred patients with emergency facilities for five hundred more. And most notable of all: it had a woman as chief matron!

For the rounding off of Simon van der Stel's image as a Rosicrucian Brother, or at least a strong sympathiser, two final aspects of the man's conduct at the Cape remain to be discussed. Both are revealed by eye-witnesses.

The first is referred to by an implacable enemy of Van der Stel. Why the German naturalist-astronomer-author Peter Kolbe, a frequent visitor to the Governor's country estate Constantia, hated his host so much, has never been adequately explained. Perhaps it was the German's arrogance and pedantry that put Simon's hair up and led him to pull Kolbe's leg with fantastic stories about his expedition to Namaqualand "where the moon was so close to the earth that he had touched it", thereby inspiring his victim's total lack of a sense of humour. In any case, we are indebted to this German scientist for revealing some facts about life at Constantia that no other source ever mentioned. One day arriving unexpectedly at the beautiful gabled house, Peter Kolbe saw on a table three books — the Koran, the Ethics by Spinoza and The Jewish War by Flavius Josephus. Although he told many lies about Van der Stel, these three titles could hardly have been the fruit of a malicious imagination and we may take it that those books were really there. That a Dutch colonial governor who had to sit each Sunday (probably twice) in the front pew of the Dutch Reformed Church, was a reader of the Koran is, to put it mildly, puzzling, but that he was a student of Spinoza's Ethics is even more intriguing. Without alleging that Spinoza was a member of the Rosicrucian Brotherhood in the Netherlands or at least a fellow-traveller, it is clear that specifically in his Ethics many thoughts were developed which were related to contemporary Rosicrucian thinking. His thesis that free, unhampered thinking — 'philosophising' he called it — was the right of every human being, went directly against the teachings of the

48

established churches. Worse: Spinoza's understanding of the Kabala and his elaborating on this forbidden esoteric philosophy puts him alongside Christian Rozenkreutz and his pupils, who also studied the Kabala. Consequently the fact that Van der Stel possessed a copy of the Ethics marks him as a man who, like the Rosicrucians, wanted a totally new approach to religious and specifically Christian thinking.

The second of the two final aspects of Simon van der Stel's conduct and life at the Cape of Good Hope, required to complete the Rosicrucian image, was uncovered by Ds. Francois Valentyn, world traveller and writer, who was another — much more welcome — guest at Governor Van der Stel's magnificent Constantia.

But first, let me recapitulate. From my studies of seventeenth Century Rosicrucianism in Western Europe it had become clear that a true Rosicrucian was faced with the following primary duties :

1. He had – to put it in Rudolf Steiner words – "to cultivate ancient wisdom." By studying Islam and Spinoza, Van der Stel complied with that requirement.

2. He had to perform at least one purely creative deed. Simon van der Stel did: he founded Stellenbosch.

3. He had to search for minerals and study them. By following lectures on geology at the Athenaeum in Amsterdam as a youngster, and by travelling to Namaqualand to look for copper as colonial administrator, Van der Stel amply fulfilled this third command.

4. He had to go out into the world to heal. The Cape's ambitious hospital is the main witness of the Governor's implementation of that instruction.

5. He had to purify and embellish his environment. By cleaning up dirty little Cape Town, and remodelling and improving the Company gardens, and planting oak trees wherever this could be done, Simon did so quite conspicuously.

49

Having come this far during my research for my biographical novel *Man of Constantia,* I felt not yet justified in putting the label 'Rosicrucian' on Governor Simon van der Stel. For I knew that there still was a sixth commandment, one perhaps less known to students of the Rosicrucian Brotherhood but not less important than the others:— The Rosicrucian had to read and study at least one chapter of the Bible every day of his life.

So I went back to my sources and scrutinized them again. At last I found what I was looking for in Ds Valentyn's monumental works on the Dutch East India Company, published at the beginning of the 18th Century.

Ds Valentyn visited the Cape of Good Hope twice. The second time was in 1695, a few years after Commander Van der Stel's promotion to Governor, when the homestead Constantia and its excellent wines were famous all over the civilized world. During his first visit there years earlier Ds Valentyn did not find Simon at home, because the Commander was sweating it out in hot and dry Namaqualand. This time, however, he was graciously entertained at the lovely estate. While favourably commenting on the spectacular progress the Colony had made since his previous call, the Dutch clergyman tells us a great deal about his hosts' private life.

One of Valentyn's observations — made so casually that it had earlier escaped my attention — was that the Governor had the laudable habit of making every day — mind you, every day — an illustration from a chapter of the Bible. Nobody will disagree when I put it that some-one who tries to illustrate a certain story must first study it thoroughly. And so one knows for certain that this impressive Cape Governor also complied with the sixth Rosicrucian demand.

Above all Rosicrucians were bridge builders. The great sage and initiate who founded the Brotherhood — Christian Rozenkreutz — tried to build a bridge between the spirit and matter, between the divine and the profane. His famous Dutch pupil, Johan Baptiste van Helmont, often called the foremost chemist of the 17th Century, laid the bridge between alchemy and chemistry. Wherever Rosicrucians were active — whether it was a Leibnitz in Nuremberg in science, or a Rembrandt in Amsterdam in art — they aimed at building a bridge between the Creator and this Creation: Mankind. Their hearts may have been with God in Heaven but their feet stood firmly on the ground. Christ came to our earth because God deemed this earth important enough to send His Son down to purify it. Thanks to the Rosicrucian influence this fact was accepted in 17th Century Holland to an extent never known in the Middle Ages.

In bringing permanence and beauty to a little halfway refreshment station between the Republic of the United Netherlands Provinces and its colonial empire in the Far East, Simon van der Stel also tried to build a bridge. The bridge, nowadays called the Republic of South Africa — linking the East and West — now recognised as such by the statesmen and politicians who dominate today's world scheme. It was obviously seen by Rudolf Steiner who — according to Max Stibbe — once referred to the sub-continent as a future bulwark of global civilization. It was even sharper outlined as such by the same Stibbe and that other gifted Steiner faithful, Zeylmans van Emmichoven, who both came to this part of the world to spread the gospel of Anthroposophy, and died here. These men never doubted that in a not too distant future the struggling young nation on the tip of Africa would carry out this specific function. When this happens one may thank in the first place that man of destiny, Simon van der Stel, who even in the mixture of his Dutch and Indian blood was a link between East and West. He remained at the Cape after his retirement as Governor and died at Constantia in 1712. He gave his ashes — just like his spiritual successors Zeylmans and Stibbe did — to the country he built and loved.

When one tries to fathom the spiritual meaning of laying a bridge between East and West, between Western and Eastern civilization, it soon becomes clear that in this instance the Rosicrucian concept reaches its highest expression. Standing between the prevailing Ahrimanic forces of the West and the Luciferic forces of the East, South Africa could well be the predestined place where God-the-Son would want to work to fulfil His cosmic mission of love.

Chapter 4

Lalibela

An Expression of Prester John ?

Rachael Shepherd

At THE END OF THE STORY of Parsifal as it is recounted by Wolfram von Eschenbach we are told that Repanse de Schoye, the Maiden of the Grail, becomes united with Feirefis, the half brother of Parsifal, who is a man of mixed blood and mixed race. Later in India, she gives birth to a son named Prester John, who is destined not to be just one person, but the beginning of a line of people who will bear this title.

In this statement Wolfram tells us everything and almost nothing about Prester John, and this was exactly the situation at the time of Wolfram's writing in 1212 when the name of Prester John first rang in the ears of European peoples. This was the time of the ending of the Crusades, of the powers of the Knights Templar, the time of the striving to conclude the wars against the Moors and Islam. The church at this time had become much less a spiritual force and much more a temporal power, amassing immense wealth by selling absolutions to those wealthy enough to afford them, to name but one example. The priesthood itself had become a shelter for ruffians and criminals, as reported by Peter Abelard in his famous letters to Heloise. There was no longer an ideal within the Roman Catholic Church, except for the newly formed Franciscans and the heretical sect of the Cathars where purity, goodness and Christian Brotherhood could still be experienced. It is against this background that we find the quest for the Grail and for Prester John. It was the time of Mankind's deepest descent into matter, that preceded the dawn of the new consciousness heralded by the Renaissance.

The people of Europe dreamed of the land of Prester John out of a desire to find the perfect Christian king and the land with the most perfect Christian order. They longed for an experience of this ideal in a purely personal sense but also in order to find a model for their own kingdoms, and they sought, out of necessity, a strong fellow-campaigner in the struggle against Islam. But in their questing was something else. What they sought, if they had reflected upon it, could never have been found on earth; it was a seeking for an experience of the spiritual world, but it was just this which inspired them to the voyages of discovery and which highlighted as the threshold of discovery, the Cape of Africa.

The quest for knowledge of Prester John like the quest for the person himself is tantalising in the extreme and one continually has to try to sift fact from fantasy and embellishment, but perhaps one approach is through the person with whom he is often identified and who is very intimately connected with his being, the Priest-King Lalibela of Ethiopia.

In the Gerla Lalibela, the book of The Way of Life, that was possibly written by Lalibela himself and was discovered this century in the Church of Mary in the city of Lalibela that was named after him in Ethiopia, the story of his life is told as follows:

"There was once a Priest-King of Ethiopia by the name of Zagwe who had in the course of time a son named Gophre Maria and a daughter named Orierna. But he also took a second wife, Keru Worgna of Sagota, who was the daughter of a priest-regent in the land. By this second wife, Zagwe had another son who was said to have been born at Bugna in the niche of a rock and was given the name of Lalibela, which when translated, means 'he whom the bees love.'

When Lalibela was born, the prophecy of a soothsayer said that Lalibela would one day become king, not only of his father's country but of many other lands besides including Egypt itself. This worried his step-sister considerably because she saw that the future of her real brother was thereby endangered, and so she went to a black magician who lived in a cave in the forest and obtained from him a special herb with which to poison Lalibela, so that he would not become king. Orierna put the poison into his food, but it was Lalibela's practice, though, out of love for them and not out of fear, always to feed his dog and his servant first, knowing that he depended on them for his existence. Both died from eating the poisoned food and Lalibela, feeling they had died on his behalf, decided in freedom that he would die with them.

He ate the food and subsequently died. He was buried by his half-brother and half-sister who noticed, to their consternation, that his limbs were still warm. Fearful that they might be responsible otherwise for burying him alive, they decided to leave the grave open for three days, hoping that he might die naturally. On the third day however, he rose from the grave and, far from being angry, was only filled with a deep sadness that his step-sister had gone to such lengths.

For forty years after this Lalibela journeyed through the world on his horse. He went first to Heliopolis in Egypt, the place to which the Christ child was also taken shortly after his birth, and learned there the great wisdom of the Egyptians, the wisdom of the Invisible Sun that would one day take on earthly form and be a companion of man. Lalibela left this place full of intense longing for the coming of such a One.

The next place on his journey was the Acropolis in Greece, the great Christian school of Dionysus the Areopagite, who had founded his school through the help and inspiration of Paul the Apostle. Here

Lalibela learned that the Invisible Sun had in fact already taken on earthly form, had lived and died as man and that there was a great wisdom to be learned regarding His being.

From Greece he journeyed to Babylon, the place of Zarathustra, he who taught men to distinguish good from evil, to know them both, and to know that evil cannot be cast out but must be overcome and redeemed. He left there with the utter conviction that Evil must be redeemed.

The last stop on his journey was to go to Jerusalem, a city thriving with Christians, who had come there from all over the world. He had lively exchanges with them before being taken on the final stage of his journey by the Angel Gabriel, who led him to the River Jordan and gave him a Christian baptism. As this took place it was as though the Heavens opened and Lalibela beheld the purpose of the experiences he had gained on his journey. He then found himself commissioned by Christ to build. He was told that three different sacred churches had to be constructed on the earth; the first was the Arch of the Covenant, built by Moses with a room of gold, the second was the Temple of Solomon built in wood, marble and stone, and now the third was to be ten churches which Lalibela must hew out of the rock of the earth which would stand for life.

Then, in the space of an hour, Lalibela led by the angels, found himself again in his own land. His brother, the King, had also been visited by Christ in a dream. He had asked him to sacrifice his Kingship to Lalibela. This he did and became a monk.

He was still full of fear, however, as to how it would be to meet his brother again, but Lalibela took him 'onto his mule' and the two rode away together as though they were one person.

Now it was time to be reunited with his wife, Makal Gebra, whose name means, "the one who owns the Cross on which Christ was crucified," so the angel led them to Imbeghsi, the Cave, close to the place where the Churches were to be built. For forty years Lalibela built those Churches; for ten years he made the instruments necessary for building and for thirty years he built them. When all was finished he gave up his Kingship to his nephew and became a priest. He spent the rest of his life in the Church of Mary, one of the ten he had created, and taught his people about Christianity, until one day Christ appeared to him in his glory like a column of fire and stretched out his hand to him. After that a man dressed only in skins visited him and led him out into the wilderness from where the Angel led him to Warwar where he died."

This biography which reads so much like a legend is actually the story of Lalibela's life from the point of view of his spiritual development, the story of a great man of the thirteenth century, working particularly about the year 1250 as far as can be ascertained, and a near contemporary of Thomas Aquinas, who strove like him to bring mankind a deeper understanding of Christianity.

If one looks at some of the images and symbols of his life story one may discover a great deal about what was working through him. When, for example, someone is born in the 'niche of a rock' it is the sign that he brings with him a high degree of spirituality; he is a great man. Through the name Lalibela, 'he whom the bees loved' or 'the Keeper of the Bees,' we are shown that he belongs to that group of human beings who, through the ages, in particular mystery centres of the world, for example Ephesus, have been both keepers of the bees in the physical sense but also in the sense of caring for individual human souls and for the healthy life of the community to which the individuals belong. Lalibela, as shown by his name, had the task of caring for individual Christian souls and of creating a new kind of Christian kingdom of the highest order.

At about the time of his coming of age he is poisoned by his step-sister and through this given the challenge, both personally and on behalf of his people, of transforming the spiritual inheritance of his country; of putting to rest that which was decadent and gleaning from it as fruit for the future that which could be redeemed. In doing it for Ethiopia, he did it also for the rest of Africa, because in former times this country stood in a sense for the whole of Africa.

What was this past of Ethiopia? It is said by Rudolf Steiner that when Old Atlantis came to an end there rose out of the Mercury

Oracles of southern Atlantis a race of men formed by the working together of the Spirits of Form, the Elohim, and the retarded spirits of the planet Mercury. When in Post-Atlantean times a place was sought for these people on the earth, present day Ethiopia was chosen as being the most suitable and they were called in fact the Ethiopians. The mysteries of the snake out of which Lalibela's sister came were a relic of that time. Still today many African tribes experience the incarnation of their tribal spirit in the form of a snake as is depicted for example in 'The African Child' by Camara Laye.

But Ethiopia had also been peopled considerably by immigrants from India who brought with them the essence of that spiritual life and culture. It had been peopled by the Arabians and the Queen of Sheba, an Arabian Queen who was also known as Makedda of Ethiopia. And it had been peopled by many Jews, particularly in the time of Solomon, who reportedly even brought with them the Arc of the Covenant. It had been ruled for a time also by some of the greatest of Egyptian Pharaohs like Hatshepsut, Ramses III and Thutmosis. In his sleep of death Lalibela digested and redeemed the good essence from all of this as seed of a new future for his country and Africa.

This sleep embarked him upon a journey on horseback lasting forty years that led him through all the major centres of world development. In the language of the spirit, the horse is the symbol of intelligence. It was with this part of his being that Lalibela took in all he encountered, and to a degree that only a man who lived at the peak of the Age of Intelligence could do. Rudolf Steiner indicates that it was only during the year 1250 that particular spiritually enlightening forces of the highest order could enter men on earth.

When, after forty years of wandering and learning, Lalibela came to his baptism in the Jordan there was a certain parallel between his destiny and that of the Jewish people who journeyed for forty years to the Promised Land, and the life of Christ Himself who also journeyed through many centres of learning in preparation for His baptism. The number Forty is the number of complete transformation and metamorphosis whether of a person, a race or an idea. The baptism in the Jordan was Lalibela's initiation into Christianity, an initiation where he was put to death and raised again, not through the rod of the Hierophant as in the pre-Christian mysteries, but through the Angel of the Lord as an inner experience. And in this moment he received his life's mission.

One can really wonder about the connection between the Arc of the Covenant, the Temple of Solomon and the Ten Churches Lalibela was to create. The first two, the Arc of the Covenant and the Temple of Solomon, were architectural structures which were essential, on the one hand for the actual incarnation of the Christ Spirit into a human body, and on the other as a home for the Ten Commandments which were destined to shape every Jewish soul from within and to build a true morality as a foundation for later Christian life. In the ten churches which together also constitute a unity, a kind of Ten-in-One, there is a certain metamorphosis of this; that which was hidden within has become an outer thing and has been planted into the earth's surface. Each of the churches contained a tabernacle with the Commandments written inside. It was an expression too of Christ's words at His Farewell discourses recorded in St. John's Gospel where he said the Ten Commandments of old must give way to the one New Commandment, that of Love, but in the one, the ten are still contained. One could say that the form of this remarkable city of Lalibela was this new commandment.

Lalibela's brother had meanwhile also been visited by Christ in a dream, and as a result of this had renounced his throne. Lalibela's gesture of taking him onto his own mule and riding away with him as one being is perhaps a statement of his willingness to share his life and its spiritual fruits with him from now on and so to found a Christian spiritual brotherhood.

One of the most intriguing elements of the biography is his journey at the end to Warwar. An examination of this name has shown that its root is connected to the word "vac" which Rudolf Steiner speaks of as the archetypal creative sound, that from which all things come forth. It is therefore a journey to the heights of the spiritual world.

This note at the end of Lalibela's life above all indicates the intimacy of his connection to that which is Johannine. It was especially in the mystery experience of Ephesus which John the Evangelist at the end of his life made a part of his own Christianity that men experienced the sphere of the World-Creating Word, the logos.

In his lecture cycle on the Gospel of St. John given in Hamburg in 1908, Rudolf Steiner speaks of the seven stages of Christian initiation that first arise for man through the consciousness of John, and which can lead to a meeting with Christ in the Spirit. They constitute an initiation of the feeling life of man and are clearly expressed in the life of Lalibela. It is perhaps this above all which indicates his connection to the John being and the possible overshadowing of Lalibela by Prester John.

On this path of Christian initiation the first stage is that of the Washing of the Feet. In its archetypal form in the life of Christ it was a deed arising out of the knowledge that although the kingdoms of plant, animal and man lie below man's stage of development man is nevertheless dependent upon them for his life and well-being, and out of this awareness man would wish to serve them. Lalibela was born in a niche of a rock; the sign that he ranked above others spiritually. Through his name Lalibela, we see him as one whose task it is to care for others, and through the fact that he always gave food first to his dog and his servant we find this first stage of the Washing of the Feet is made manifest.

The second stage is that of the Scouring. Christ suffered this in sorrow but He also saw the "necessity" of it and therefore was silent and courageous in His suffering. Lalibela endures his poisoning in a similar way, sorrowful only that his sister should resort to such a thing.

The third stage is that of the crowning with thorns, an experience of the most terrible mockery, which Christ endured because he carried an ideal so great that everything else was irrelevant beside it. The life of Lalibela tells us he too endured terrible suffering on his journey through the world but that this was irrelevant for him beside the dimension of the ideal toward which he strove.

The fourth stage is the Bearing of the Cross, of the weight of the vehicle of His destruction, of the cause of His suffering, in another

60

sense, of the weight of the physical body. Lalibela seemingly did not fulfill this stage personally but it is expressed in the name of his wife. "She who owns the Cross on which Christ was crucified." This is not explained in the story, it remains a mystery, yet St. Matthew's Gospel tells how Simon of Cyrene bore the Cross for Christ. Is it perhaps an indication that Lalibela and his wife went this spiritual path intimately together?

The fifth stage is that of the Mystic Death, for Christ the moment of the most intense inner and outer darkness followed by a sight of the spiritual world in all the glory of its lightness. This was also Lalibela's experience at his baptism, and in that moment his real task was given to him.

The sixth stage is that of being Laid in the Grave, the realisation that mankind and the earth are in a state of most intense suffering and the willingness to take on this suffering with them and on their behalf. It was to a cave, a place like a grave, that Lalibela and his wife were led by the Angel in order to begin their task of building. It was not to his own glory, satisfaction or other personal need that he built the churches but in order to alleviate the sufferings of men, to help them find their way to the Christ in His true form.

The seventh stage is the Ascension, the sight of such heights of spirit as cannot really be grasped by human perception and thinking. When Christ appeared beckoningly to Lalibela in the Church at the end of his life, and later when he was led by the Angel of Christ to the realm of the Creative Logos, he was also a part of this experience.

Was it perhaps that European people of the late Middle Ages sensed that somewhere in the world there was a monarch who had achieved such a degree of Christianity by following this Johannine path, that they called him John and longed to experience his wisdom themselves?

If one tries in conclusion to place him back in the framework of the world situation of the time it is perhaps relevant to do it in connection with the threefold path of the Knights Templar. On the first stage of their path they had, one might say, to become a Peter; to know what it means to deny in order to really know what it means to believe, in order to come to belief.

61

On the second they had in the same sense to become a James, a St. Iago, he who, on a white horse, led the Christian troops in their fight against the Moors. This experience of St. Iago on a white horse was one had by Christians and Moors alike. At this stage the Templar Knights had to learn to weather storm, chaos and the utmost disruption in order to really find and understand hope. They learned to overcome storm through the power of hope. Was it not this experience which lay behind the changing of the name of the Cape of Storms to the Cape of Good Hope? Its rounding had intimately to do with the victory of the Christians over the Moors, which was the battle of the age.

The third stage for them was to become a John, to learn at the highest level what it means to love in a new way, free of blood ties, free of sentimentality, simply out of the recognition of the Christ in man, and to express this particularly in the sphere of economics. This can happen when the economic life is based upon Brotherhood and not on competition as it now is which is by nature anti-social and therefore destructive. To achieve this stage of development the way is again through the most intense possible experience of the opposite, of utter catastrophe in life. We must round the Cape of Catastrophe in order to find the realm of John, the realm of love.

This last step was hardly begun by the Templars, perhaps because their mission was cut short, perhaps because the catastrophe of the world was not yet great enough, but they certainly were well into the quest for the kingdom of John, the realm of love, and made their way to it, perhaps instinctively, round the Cape of Africa. This Cape has won for itself the name of Hope. Does it perhaps also have a significant part to play in the experience of Catastrophe and its transformation into the experience of Love?

Chapter 5

Prester John and the Voyages of Discovery

A Search For True Community

Ralph Shepherd

THE STORIES AND LEGENDS surrounding the fabulous king-dom and personage of Prester John are linked with the legends of King Arthur and the Round Table, Parzival, the quest for the Holy Grail and the lost paradise of Shamballah. They were all set down in writing between the 10th and 13th centuries when knighthood and chivalry had reached their zenith in Europe. They also came at a time when the Holy Roman Church became much more of a worldly force in the social and political life of Europe.

These times also saw the institution of the Office of the "Holy" Inquisition and the crusades against the Cathars (the later development of the Manichean religion) who, during the later Middle Ages in southern France, were the only real opposition to the Church in Rome. With the exception of the Roman Catholic Church, the Cathars were the only organised church at that time. Until they were exterminated by the sword and the pyre. Not just thousands, but hundreds of thousands, were to die because they believed, but believed differently. The early 14th century was to see the same treatment measured out to the Knights Templars.

It was difficult then as it is today for the poor and illiterate to understand the vast wealth and the ongoing cruelty of the Roman Church in the Middle Ages, considering that it extolled the virtues of poverty and goodness. Understandably it was then that the stories of the quest for the Grail where the knights are really good, and holy men really holy, found willing ears to hear them. For nobles and peasants alike, it was comforting and inspiring to hear of the wonderful realm of Prester John where poverty and suffering had been overcome. Yet these stories were more than just a comfort, there was a certain reality about them. Even today a faint echo arises from the depths of our souls that in some quiet, almost imperceptible way, says: "Yes, they are true" to places like Shamballah, the Paradise Lost, or the Logres of King Arthur. "Somewhere they exist," these strange, mythical realms like the Forest of Brocelinde of Parzival, or the Realm of Prester John.

The stories of Prester John's kingdom began to filter back to Europe from the Near East, with the returning crusaders. They told of a humble and just king with an immense realm somewhere in the East or in one of the Indies (Ethiopia and other regions of Africa were also called India by the Europeans of that time).[1]

This king whose name was John was also a priest of the Christian faith, hence the name, Prester John.

Some of the tales place Prester John as one of the descendants of the magi who, according to St. Matthew's Gospel, visited the Christ child with their gifts of gold, frankincense and myrrh. Others identified Prester John with John the Evangelist who Christ said would not die until He returned. As Christ had not yet returned, this Prester John was surely John the Evangelist for he never seemed to age.

His court was said to be so large that he was served by 72 kings, numerous princes, bishops, dukes and many other nobles.[2] Prester John's humility was such that he saw himself only as a servant of Christ and therefore a servant of humanity. He rode a lowly mule whilst his servants rode great horses. To emphasise his piousness, he had chosen the title of priest, and, as mentioned already, was to be called Prester John.

From this point, the stories move out of the realm of the physical and into a fantastic world of magical beasts and strange imagery. Prester John's table was said to be cut from a single emerald and stands on two pillars of amethyst, seating 30 000 people. The mighty and the lowly are fed together at this great table. In this land there are no poor, and there is work for all. Also in his court was said to be a magic mirror through which Prester John could see into every corner of his 72 provinces. His robes are woven by salamanders (fire spirits) and are washed in fire.

There were also many marvellous beasts in this land, including the first known reference to the Unicorn. In the legend of the Kingdom of Prester John the unicorn and the lion are in continual conflict. It is from this legend that the lion and the unicorn on the British coat of arms have their origin. There they are no longer in conflict, however, but mutually supporting the shield and insignia of Great Britain. When James VI of Scotland came to the English throne as James I in 1603, he redesigned the royal arms replacing the red dragon of Wales with a white unicorn from the royal arms of Scotland, to support the shield.[3]

However, the first official mention of Prester John is by the historian, Bishop Otto of Freising, reporting on a meeting he had witnessed between Bishop Hugh of Jabala in the Holy Land and Pope Eugenius III. This meeting took place at Viterbo in central Italy in November 1145. Bishop Hugh was seeking papal support for the second crusade. The Muslim threat to the Christian states in the Holy Land had grown to such proportions that nothing short of another crusade would help against the overwhelming odds that faced the small groups of Christians settled in the Near East. The second crusade did take place but was such a fiasco that the Christian states were left in a worse plight than before.

Bishop Hugh related to the Pope the fall of the City of Edessa to the Moors, and the general plight of the Christians in the near East. He then told the story of how a priest-king called John, a Christian, made war on the Muslim city of Ecbatana. The city was defended by Medeans, Persians and Assyrian forces, but the three-day battle saw Prester John emerge victorious. After this, Prester John moved his vast army to assist the Christians in Jerusalem. Unfortunately, the army could find no way of crossing the Tigris so, after some years, Prester John was forced to return home. It appears that Bishop Hugh's main reason for relating this story to the Pope was to dispel the idea that help could be sought from other quarters, i.e. Prester John.

This report of Bishop Otto of Freising implicitly shows how well known the legends of Prester John were in those times. Modern historians have discovered that the battle described by Bishop Hugh did in fact take place and have identified it with the defeat of Sanjar, the Seljuk Turkish ruler of Persia, by the army of the empire of Kara-Kitai in 1141. This Chinese-Mongolian empire followed a blend of Christianity and Buddhism, closely identified with Manicheism. It was easy to see then how physical and spiritual events can play into each other. The next official report of Prester John supposedly came from his own hand. In 1165, a letter written in Latin and addressed to the Byzantine Emperor Manuel Comenus, was circulated in Europe. Ronald Latham says in his introduction to The Travels of Marco Polo, that "Thanks to this letter, which soon became a best seller, every European traveller in the East was on the look-out for Prester John 'of whose great empire all the world speaks'" (p.93). In the years and centuries that were to follow, more and more copies of this letter were to be found throughout Europe, each letter containing further embellishments of more wondrous and strange beasts and men; although the original letter itself was probably written by Harbey the half-brother of King Lalibela of Ethiopia (circa 1200). Harbey and Lalibela were not of the Solomonic line but belonged to the usurper dynasty of the Zagwes.[4] However fantastic, and for whatever reason the letter was written, the letter still inspired adventurers and scholars alike to find the kingdom of Prester John. Wolfram von Eschenbach in his classical Grail story *Parzival*, written circa 1207, makes Prester John the son of Repanse de Schoye and Feirefis, the half-brother of Parzival. The mother of Feirefis is Belacane, a black queen from Africa or India.

By the end of the 14th Century Prester John's kingdom had become much more identified with Africa than with Asia, and with Ethiopia in particular. A century before, Marco Polo completed his travels through Asia and made references to his own search for Prester John[5] who he identified with one of the Khans of the Mongolian steppes, many of whom were Manichean or Nestorian Christians.

A Genoese cartographer, Giovanni da Carignano, who was active in map making from 1291 to 1329, was the first authority to affirm that Prester John's kingdom was in Africa and not in India as was sometimes assumed.[6]

Of all the countries and peoples who were fired with the zeal to search for Prester John, it was Portugal which at the forefront of general European advancement in launching the Voyages of Discovery was to lead the search for this Christian Kingdom of harmony and peace.

Queen Philippa, the English-born wife of King John I of Portugal, organised the first military expedition to create an overland route to the land of Prester John. In August 1415, a small force of 45 000 men sailed from Lisbon under the command of Duarte, Pedro and Henry, three of the five sons of John and Philippa. They successfully captured the port of Ceuta in the Kingdom of Fez on the African coast. But this conquest only proved to the Portuguese that there was no possibility of carving a land route across Africa to Prester John. The vastness of the Sahara Desert and the ferocity of the Moors would render any attempt to reach the eastern part of Africa futile. If a way was to be found, it would have to be a sea route around Africa.

Philippa's son Henry, later known as Henry the Navigator, made the task of finding a sea route to Prester John his life's mission. Born in 1394,[7] Henry's greatest avowed ambition was "To have knowledge of the land of Prester John."[8] At the age of 18, Henry was inducted as the Grand Master of the Order of Christ.

At the request of King Dinis of Portugal (1279–1325) to establish the Order of Christ, in the previous century, Pope John XXII imposed upon its knights the rule of St. Benedict and the Constitution of Citeaux. Prince Henry submitted himself to them completely with body, soul and spirit. He adopted celibacy and lived a very austere life with no physical comforts, even adopting a hair shirt and gravel bed. His whole being was directed to the service of the spirit.

In order to make what were later known as the Voyages of Discovery, Henry not only had to design new ships that could tack against the wind, but he had to invent navigation as well. It was through the Order of Christ that the voyages of discovery were made possible, but what was this Order of Christ?

Through the instigation of Philip the Fair of France (1285–1314), Pope Clement V dissolved the Order of the Knights Templar on 22 March 1312. An Order of Dissolution was dispatched throughout Europe and the immense wealth of the Templars was confiscated. Much of this wealth was seized by kings and nobles and particularly by Philip the Fair. What little was left in the remaining possessions was to be transferred to the Hospitalers.

King Dinis of Portugal, was a secret supporter of the Knights Templar, so when he received the order of dissolution from the Pope, he sent the Knights into hiding and only made a show of confiscating their possessions. After reporting this to the Pope, he requested that he might form his own order to protect the church's (and his own) interests as well as providing a military force to fight the Moors. In the meantime, both Philip the Fair and Clement V had died and Pope John XXII now sat in the Chair of St. Peter. This request was granted. Dinis recalled the Templars, investing them with the new Order of Christ, and gave them back their possessions.

The Order of Christ was therefore a continuation of the Order of the Templars. The full title of the Templars was the Order of the Poor Knights of Christ of the Temple of Solomon. Now they no longer held Jerusalem from their seat at the Temple, neither were they poor, so Dinis rightly simply called them The Order of Christ.

At the height of their activities the Templars had over 3 000 depositories or banks between London and Jerusalem.

Inspired to search for the kingdom of Prester John where a new Christianity was said to exist, founded upon universal brotherhood and the Gospel of St. John, Henry the Navigator was able to make use of the wealth of the Order of Christ to finance his plans. Later it was necessary that the voyages of discovery became self-financing, and this was achieved by the development of trade with Africa and India.

At the beginning of his work, Henry established a centre for research on a promontory known as Cape Sagres in South-West Portugal. It was here that he built a small town. He lived the life of an ascetic studying the works of geographers from all lands, yet he also met and conferred with all manner of travellers, gathering comprehensive information wherever he could on science, astronomy, mathematics, ship building but particularly about the shape of the world and the eastern Atlantic. At Sagres, Henry developed a school for navigation and for preparing the sailors inwardly for what they were to encounter on their travels. In those times it was generally believed that if a boat sailed too far south or west, it would sail off the edge of the world. Materialistic thinking stands in a similar light today in its adherence to a cartesian world outlook.[9]

Dr. Georg Unger of the General Anthroposophical Society in Dornach, Switzerland, worked with American astronauts during the early 1960's to prepare them mentally for facing the then unknown conditions of space. His task was to prepare the astronauts to be able to control their thinking processes in an environment where there was no light, sound nor gravity. The normal involuntary response to such a condition is to become unconscious. Unger developed meditative exercises from the work of Rudolf Steiner that effectively combated this condition. Henry the Navigator had a similar task in preparing the seamen of his age to overcome fear and to develop trust. To spend a year or two at sea in a vessel about the size of a harbour tug took a courage and fortitude that is not easy to appreciate in today's world of giant tankers and jet travel.

Sagres was in a sense a school of initiation, also of research and development and of scientific education. It was upon this foundation that the Voyages of Discovery were to begin. Unfortunately little is known about the research and methods employed by Henry due to the enforced security surrounding his work. Transgressions were punished by death.[10]

Henry was not to see the fulfilment of his work for he died in 1460, having completed all that was necessary for the new step in the development of European consciousness, the opening of Europe to the whole world. Within the next century, first Portuguese ships and then others circumnavigated the world.

Henry's plan was to find the Realm of Prester John and thus bring a renewal of Christianity to Europe, to conquer the Muslims and establish a harmony among peoples. Sadly, the new Christianity was not yet to be found. The European consciousness was far too immature for the development opened by Henry the Navigator. Instead of following spiritual impulses and thereby taking a new consciousness as an offering to the New World, the European sea-farers raped and pillaged it. Cortez was the first of the Europeans who were responsible for conquering the world in the most brutal and savage way possible. Glorified by many as the age of the great conquests of Europe, it only came to a close with the almost complete extermination of the American Red Indians and the Australian aborigines in the 19th century.

South Africa was to be one of the few places on earth where settlement by Europeans was done without mass slaughter.

Bartolomeo Dias was the first to round the Cape of Africa in 1488. So great was the storm as he reached the Cape in his small vessel, that he was driven right around the Cape without being aware of it. When eventually the storm abated, he discovered to his great joy that he had in fact rounded it. Dias did not travel much further up the coast of Africa and after passing Algoa Bay, he turned about and headed homewards. Dias and his men were to see on their return the mighty headland which he named the Cape of Storms. Upon his return to Portugal, King John II renamed it the Cape of Good Hope, in recognition of the fact that the power of hope of the sailors had already overcome something of the storm and tempest. Nine years were to pass before the next main voyage which was to take Vasco da Gama around the Cape and on to India.

The sailing of Vasco da Gama from Portugal on the 8th July 1497 was preceded by solemn Christian rituals during which King Manoel, who ascended to the Portuguese throne after the death of John II, invested Da Gama with the mission to discover the Realm of Prester John and the route to India. This journey was under the auspices of the Order of Christ. During the ceremony, Vasco da Gama was given the silk flag of the Order, an eight-pointed Red Cross on a white background. Da Gama himself held a leading position in the Order of Christ.

The portraits we have of him show him with the cross of the order on his breast. Da Gama then vowed to the King that once unfurled, the flag would never again be folded and would be carried aloft and to the fore into whatever realm or land they should come in their travels. The other officers and captains, including Vasco's brother Paolo da Gama, were to swear the same oath.

At sunrise on the 8th July, the flag ship the St. Gabriel, commanded by Vasco da Gama and followed by the St. Raphael, the Berrio and a supply ship, set sail to the Eastern shores of Africa and then on to India. Henry the Navigator hoped that by opening the route to India, trading would develop that could finance the future passages to Prester John. He sent letters confirming Vasco da Gama's own ambassadorial status, beside personal letters to Prester John and the King of India. The importance of this voyage was to inspire the Portuguese poet, Camoens, to write the history of this and subsequent voyages in his classic work, The Lusiads. Da Gama, like Dias before him, experienced the most terrible storms of the Cape. Camoens describes this in his poem as the meeting with Adamastor, the foreboding spirit of the Cape. Gigantic in size and utterly fearful to see, Adamastor promises the sailors death if they should pass his threshold. This threat or curse proved to be true for the great majority of the first sailors who rounded the Cape; Vasco da Gama lost his brother through illness and later his son whilst fighting for the King of Ethiopia. Da Gama did reach India but he was not able to fulfil the task of meeting Prester John.

In the same year as the first rounding of the Cape by Dias, King John II despatched Pero da Covilha and Alfonso de Paiva overland as his ambassadors to Prester John. They made their way first to Cairo via Naples and Rhodes. Disguised as merchants, they travelled South to Aden where they parted company, having arranged to meet again in Cairo. Two years later Covilha arrived back in Cairo to discover that Paiva had arrived some time before and had died of an illness without revealing the success or failure of his quest. Covilha then met two Portuguese Jews sent by King John to find him and Paiva. Knowing now that he could not return to Portugal without attempting to reach Prester John, he travelled with one of the Jews, Rabbi Abraham, as far as Armuz. After further wanderings he eventually arrived at the Court of King Eskender of Ethiopia. Covilha was well received and cared for by the "Prester John" but discovered, like Marco Polo some centuries before, that there was little resemblance to the Prester John of the legends, no matter how grand the Court of Eskender was. Covilha was not allowed to leave the court, and when Fransisco Alvares arrived as part of the embassy of Rodrego de Lima in 1520, Covilha was still there, now married to an Ethiopian wife with a family of his own. Covilha was to die there a few years later, never knowing what had become of his wife in Lisbon and the child she was carrying 30 years before.

The priest, Francisco Alvares, wrote the first full account of the Kingdom of Prester John.[11] By this time Europe had decided that the Ethiopian emperors were the Prester Johns that so many had searched for. The Ethiopian kings in turn did not mind and some even signed their letters 'Prester John'.

Ethiopia had adopted Christianity in the 4th Century. The first

Bishop was Frumentius, a man not from Ethiopia but from Tyre in the near East. The Ethiopians called their spiritual leader 'Abba Salama' (Father of Peace).[12]

Trade and contact between Europe and Ethiopia was difficult because of the remoteness of Ethiopia and the hostility of her neighbours, yet contact and some trade did take place in the centuries preceding the arrival of the Portuguese. There is a report in the archives of Goa dated 1130 of a party of 30 Ethiopians who had come to Europe on a diplomatic mission and were now returning home through Goa.

Essentially Coptic in nature, the Ethiopians have retained without schism their Christianity until recent times. Now, under the threat of continual harassment from Islamic fundamentalists, the future of Christianity in Ethiopia is again uncertain.

During the last three decades we have seen one Christian African state after another, topple to Islam. This development is not restricted to Africa. In England, Germany and other European countries we see what were once active but now empty churches being converted to Mosques through the spread of Islam. During this same period, we have witnessed the revival of interest in the legends of the Grail, of the Knights Templar and also of Prester John. This search for esoteric Christianity was taken up by a group of theologians around the Lutheran pastor, Dr. Friederich Rittelmeyer. With the suggestions and help of Dr. Rudolf Steiner, the Movement for Religious Renewal was founded.[13] Today, under the name of The Christian Community, the church has grown and is active in most European and American countries. In South Africa there are now five centres where The Christian Community is working. This is but one example of the need and search for the 'new' Christianity. Christian orthodoxy seems unable to meet the challenge of the times in either combating scientific materialism or in developing effective Christian brotherhood. The cosmic Gospel of Christ has given way to the social and simple man, Jesus of Nazareth. It is little wonder that the liberation theology that supports violent revolution has taken such a firm hold in the Third World in particular, but in the First World as well. The new Christianity is identified with what is referred to by theologians as the

Johannine Christianity.

Seen by some as the third development of Christianity, the Johannine follows the Petrine and Pauline developments. Johannine Christianity is said to be a state in human consciousness where each individual will experience as his own, the suffering of his fellow man. It is to develop empathy to the point where the human soul can reach into and carry the sufferings of another in order to alleviate their pain.

Sympathy is the forerunner of empathy and was (and still is) the work of Pauline Christianity — to develop the experience of sympathy through the practice of sermonising without the ritual of the Petrine Church. Empathy, on the other hand, is the real experience of the sufferings of another as though they were one's own.

Christianity, however, is Christianity. Its seeming division into three types are only divisions into stages of consciousness. The stages of consciousness themselves have no spiritual advantage. It is just as easy for a Johannine Christian to fall into sin as it is for a Petrine Christian.

The forerunners of Johannine Christianity were the Rosicrusians, a secret esoteric group of Christians (secret because they had no wish to be burnt at the stake), that developed in Europe almost parallel with the development of Pauline Christianity by Luther and Calvin.

In our age we can be open (in the Western world at least) with our beliefs. The great mass of material, some of it pure dilettantism, some of it very valuable and based upon esoteric truths that has appeared in libraries and bookshops in the past three decades, is evidence not just of a re-awakening to spiritual realities but of a new consciousness in mankind. The physical Voyages of Discovery, inaugurated by Henry the Navigator, are now being replaced by spiritual voyages of discovery. As Henry had to discover Navigation which has its own rules and laws, and without which the sailors could never have embarked upon their journeys, so too in our time is it necessary to discover the rules and laws pertaining to the spiritual world. In this century it is the spiritual scientists like Rudolf Steiner, who have discovered those rules and laws upon which spiritual journeys of discovery can now take place.

74

South Africa was discovered by those "en route" to Prester John, the Knights Templar with a new name, and financed by Templar wealth. The Order of Christ christened the Cape by their victory over storm and tempest, the Cape of Good Hope. Then on Christmas Day 1497 they christened the land they found on that day, Natal (the Place of Birth).

The Realm of Prester John has not yet been found, and may never be found on earth, but maybe it can still be reached by those who can develop the spiritual strength and the spiritual sight to see into the Realm of Prester John and bring back the spiritual gifts that may take mankind on the next step towards its spiritual home.

There is no doubt that the Realm of Prester John does exist, but the road to it is still being sought.

With the new laws for spiritual navigation now available to those wishing to make the journey, maybe we will not have to wait too long before the real treasures from the Realm of Prester John may be shared.

REFERENCES

1   *The Caravels of Christ* by Gilbert Rhinolith. George Allen and Unwin. 1959.

2   *The Realm of Prester John* by Robert Silverberg. Doubleday and Company. 1972.

3   *Ibid.*

4   *The Sign and the Seal*, by Graham Hancock. Mandarin 1993, page 105.

5   *The Travels* by Marco Polo translated by Ronald Latham. Penguin Books. 1958.

6   *The Sign and The Seal* by Graham Hancock. Mandarin 1993, page 161.

7   *Ibid.*, p 168

8   *Ibid.*, p 170

9   *The Turning Point* by Fritjof Capra. Flamingo Books. 1986.

10 *The Sign and The Seal* by Graham Hancock. Mandarin 1993, page 170.

11 *The Prester John of the Indies* translated by Lord Stanley or Alderley, revised and edited by C.F. Beckingham and G.W.B. Huntingford.

12 *The Abyssinians* by David Buxton, Thames and Hudson. 1970.

13 *Growing Point.* Dr. Alfred Heidenreich. Floris Books. 1984.

Chapter 6

The Eastern King

Evelyn Francis Capel

How do we find our heroes? Once upon a time the crown was the symbol, but even today most little children in the kindergarten are happy to wear a cardboard crown. The statue of Richard the Lion Heart still presides over the houses of Parliament in London, from outside. But far back in history, in the Middle Ages and earlier, the crown was a symbol of mystical power. It bestowed the authority of a hero on those who wore it. Even when, in the seventeenth century, Cromwell, as president of the country in England, ordered the beheading of King Charles the First, it is said that he never again slept an easy sleep until he died. The monarchy was of course restored in Britain, but the glory of the crown had gone.

But the heroic kings of earlier times belonged to mythology more than history. They carried a divinity in their being through which they became heroes for many centuries. They were human and divine at the same time. Their proportions were those of demi-gods. Their reputation lasted for centuries. The places named after them became sanctuaries. There were three great Kings with this quality in the early times of Europe and they were heroes by right of their divinity. It came about that King Arthur had the reputation of not having died, but of having been laid to rest in the Isle of Avalon, in a deep sleep from which he could always be wakened when his kingdom of Britain would need him again. This could be said of a hero of mythology, but it also became a factor in history. King Arthur was the hero of the West; Parzival of the centre of Europe; and the most mysterious of all — Prester John — of the East. They were heroes with qualities of the spiritual nature revealed in them and through which they led their people in the trials of history.

Curiously enough, it was not their achievements through which they became lasting heroes, far from an outer point of view, they might have seemed like failures. They were honoured for ideals and aims, which are still as much in the future as they were in previous times. Their reputations lasted so long, that in our modern age their very existence has been doubted. Through the intervention of Winston Churchill, King Arthur has been given again a historical existence. But the other kings await their champions. Yet their ideals and aims have not faded away and can still inspire, even if their history is questioned. Nowadays, our heroes are expected to be part of history and they are elevated to a place in mythology after they have died out of the historical circumstances. But for earlier ages the situation was different and the mythological hero had chief place reigning over centuries of time. Ideals were sent down into history through the hero kings, but each of them came down once into Earth in human form and carried the myth into outer history. In this sense, King Arthur belongs to the West Country in Britain. He had a castle which was also his temple of the Mysteries in Tintagel. The round table represented a sanctuary, its twelve seats stood for the Signs of the Zodiac. The knights had their annual instruction and inspiration each year at Whitsuntide. They aimed at establishing on Earth the sacred kingdom of Logres, where the wisdom of the Stars would direct the social life of the people on the Earth. In earthly form, the Round Table was broken up and the betrayal by the false knight which brought about the defeat of Arthur in battle. But the coming again of Arthur never ceased to be the great hope of his people and their descendants through the years. That which occupied a little piece of history on Earth returned to mythology to be the great hope of the future.

The legend of King Parzival was also reproduced once in earthly history. His famous journey, alone and unaided, was represented in the country of the Vosges mountains and the legend was taken up by the poets, who spread it far and wide in their songs. In modern times Tennyson has taken into his poetry the myths of King Arthur, and still earlier, Von Eschenbach took up the myth of Parzival into literature. But the legends of Prester John did not reach a satisfactory incarnation. Christianity early spread into the world in the East and Prester John was considered to have had his kingdom there. The tyrants who conquered in China, suppressed Christianity in favour of Islam. Legends of Prester John in India still survive, but in terms of mythology. In later times, in the fifteenth century, the kingdom was moved from India to Africa. The legend became connected with a piece of history in Ethiopia. A long time earlier, the Queen of Sheba left her country beside the Red Sea, and travelled to Jerusalem to learn the high wisdom of Solomon. The result of her journey was that she had a son, who so much resembled Solomon, that his people wished to make him king. A little crowd of Princes joined him and they set out to form a country of their own. They arrived in Ethiopia in North Africa, bringing with them by stealth the tablets of stone on which the Laws of Moses were written. These they deeply revered. Later on, an early form of Christianity was taken up in Ethiopia and it was regarded as a Christian country. A sacred history called the Nebra gave the mystical right of the emperors of Ethiopia to become Christian emperors. But the country was never at peace and in the time of Queen Victoria, a British army arrived in Ethiopia. The commander of the expedition discovered the emperor's palace and found the Emperor himself lying in bed, murdered. Under his pillow was a mysterious document. According to the accepted custom of the time, the book was taken away and presented to the British Museum in London. Still later, Queen Victoria received a sad letter from a younger and later emperor, begging her to return the sacred book, for it was the symbol of his authority in his own kingdom. Queen Victoria had much sympathy for distressed monarchs and she prevailed upon the Trustees of the British Museum to return the manuscript, after it had been copied. Before that time an adventurous Portuguese had taken a journey to Ethiopia and written an account of his experiences. He confirmed the conviction of his people, but was made very unhappy by the peculiar customs and theology that was called 'Christian' among the Ethiopians. It became the custom for those who supported the theology of the Ethiopian church to speak of the Emperor as Prester John, thereby moving him from China through India, to Ethiopia.

In reality, the myth of Prester John did not descend into earthly history the same way as that of King Arthur and King Parzival. But into modern times the kingdom of Prester John has been held to be a genuine part of the Christian Church. In the time of the Crusades, when they were conducted by people of great mystical faith and very little information about the physical world, the hope was very important that the crusades would find, behind the armies of their un-Christian enemies, a holy, Christian kingdom with which they could unite. It is embodied in a certain document of high value, in which a Christian Emperor beseeches another one in Ethiopia, to go to the help of the crusaders from behind the armies of their enemies. At that period in history, the thought of Prester John, a Christian Emperor in the East, was a great source of the courage with which the crusaders pressed on to Jerusalem. In one sense, the myth had descended into history, but the few people of the time who entered Ethiopia, as the Portugese monk had done, were doubtful about the Christian practices they had encountered.

Every year, in the middle of the winter, the emperor and his bishops received a baptism of the whole body in the clear water running down from the melting snow in the high mountains. They felt a necessity to renew their original Baptism in this way. Right into this century, the last Emperors of Ethiopia were accepted in the world as representatives of the Christian Church.

Beyond the outer history of the legend of Prester John, stands the inner meaning, the spiritual aim, which it represents. There is, so says the legend, a holy temple which is the dwelling of Prester John. His companions and his servants are all bishops, or dignitaries of the Church. His dwelling is a temple, where the Sacraments are continually celebrated. No wrong and no sickness is allowed to be present. No redemption is needed, because there is no sin. In the mysteries of Prester John each year at mid-summer the revelation of Christianity is renewed. In the temple itself, the apostle Thomas enters as a priest celebrating the Sacraments. Each time the whole temple renews its glow of holy light, and Thomas appears, stretching out before him, the holy finger which once touched the risen body of Christ. The central Mystery protected by Prester John is the secret of the Resurrection of the body guarded and continued in the temple where the original, human, bodily nature of man is preserved in its purity. The ideal cared for and continued in this kingdom is that of Man as a spiritual being, created by the Father God, untouched by the Fall of Man, united with the new revelation of Man resurrected. St Thomas appears to confirm and strengthen the Mystery of Man's resurrection, as it appears in Christ. The kingdom devoted to the care of this Mystery is not an earthly one. The vision of Prester John is protected from the influences of fallen Mankind in a world beyond the natural, physical one around us. This Mystery is practised and protected. The time has not come when the impulses of Prester John can be brought out of its cosmic security. When the Mystery of the Resurrection is better understood and more respected in human hearts, it will descend out of its holy place into the human world and begin to work, not as a myth only, but in the realm of history. The ideals of King Arthur are sheltered in the heart of one who is asleep, ready to wake in time of need.

The Mystery of King Parzival is hidden in the heart of those inspirers of history, who are ready to work as the inner development of the human heart continues. The Mystery of Prester John is still sheltered in Paradise, but receives visitations from the apostle Thomas, until the time when Prester John can enter more clearly the evolving of human history.

The temple of Prester John is the holy place where the vision of Saint Thomas is repeated year by year. He is the apostle who in the

Christian tradition is called the doubter. By rights, he should be called the questioner instead. Thomas did not doubt, he put the question to the risen Christ, through which a higher revelation was shown of life rising out of death. Like other stories in the Gospels, no explanation is given of the strange story of Thomas. How did it happen that he was the one apostle absent at the first experience of the risen Christ by the apostles. Why had he left the upper room? Each reader of the Gospels must answer this question for himself. But it would be possible to imagine that Thomas had visited the empty tomb of which the women had given their account, and become fascinated by the questions that arose in his heart. In each account of Easter morning, it is said that the faithful women were the first to go into the garden. When they had found the tomb empty, they went off to tell the apostles. Each one who thereafter visited the tomb was faced with a problem of faith. Each one must wonder in his own way. Those who were gathered in the upper room that evening could accept that the tomb was empty because they had found the presence of Christ again, not in the garden, but in the upper room, where they had gathered for the Last Supper. It is artistically impossible to imagine that Thomas had been unable to leave the tomb in the garden, because it had become for him a problem that he could not solve.

What had the other apostles who met in the upper room, actually encountered? There is no sign in that account that Thomas doubted that the other apostles had seen Him, but one can see that it was reasonable for him to ask questions about what in fact they had seen. At that time in history, meetings with the souls of those who had died in the form of visions, were less unusual than they are now. Those can be passing experiences, like living dreams and Thomas may well have been concerned whether such dreams would have been meant by Jesus Christ in His prophesies of the Resurrection. His questioning could have been much more an enquiring in the scientific sense, of a type that could be understood today. He did not ask after visions and experiences of feeling, but he was enquiring where the meeting with the Risen One touched the realm of physical fact. He was not prepared to trust the evidence of his eyes, or the evidence of the eyes of other apostles, he asked for facts available to the sense of touch. His fellow apostles had been convinced by a great experience, which filled their hearts and comforted them with new hope. Thomas dared to say that this was not enough, but the Resurrection must be a fact, not only heartfelt, but available to the thinking mind. Everyone who seeks to understand the Resurrection will need to experience the questioning of Thomas. It opens the mind to thoughts and feelings bringing not comfort, but truth.

That this was the true question of Thomas is confirmed in St John's Gospel by his answer to the invitation of Christ to stretch out his hand and touch. The words of the Gospel do not say whether, in reality, he touched or not. But each reader is left to answer that question for himself. Thomas is said to have replied: "My Lord and my God." Whether or not he had earlier recognised the Son of God in Jesus, is not said, but in that great moment his reply is spoken to God Himself. That the Resurrection could only be the work of God, a divine act of creation taking place on Earth, is unmistakable. The strongest knowledge of the Resurrection expressed in the words of the Gospel is Thomas's own answer to his original question. Within the Mysteries cared for by Prester John this one lives on which was initiated by the apostle Thomas. It is entrusted to the divine King whose temple is not really on the Earth, leading to all those who confront in Prester John the task of understanding in a deeper and higher sense what is the nature of the Resurrection.

King Arthur presided over the Mystery of the divine origin of Man among the Stars. King Parzival has opened the mystery for each human soul of the divine spirit hidden within him. Prester John calls up the Mystery of what in human history is the true meaning of the Resurrection. These are all cosmic questions requiring answers in human life on Earth. In this sense, these divine kings are heroes asking mankind where it comes from and where it is going. They inspire, but they do so with questions. Statements require belief and ask for doubt. The questions are addressed to the ability of each individual person to think for himself. They lead therefore away from dogma towards the inner experience of freedom. In the temple of Prester John, the question is raised of what responsibilities are present in human souls because they are human and because they live on Earth. The kingdom of Prester John is still hidden, while people on Earth prepare to ask the questions which are presented in the appearance of Thomas. He holds himself more aloof from the earthly life of people, because he is preparing the greatest challenge. King Arthur could ask his knights to fight evil and wrong. King Parzival could ask his followers to cross the wasteland to the lonely castle of the fisher King. Prester John invites human souls to look for the temple of the question, in which the meaning of life on Earth will be unfolded.

The mystery of Prester John is unfinished. It points to that which is of the future, to that which speaks of the coming history of mankind. The mysteries of King Arthur are unfinished. He sleeps until the Kingdom of Logres can be established in reality in the social life on Earth. The mysteries of the Grail are sheltered in the castle beyond the wasteland, until the inner life of the human mind becomes what it really is. But the kingdom of Prester John has still to descend out of the Heavens not yet revealed. Our human life on Earth is not yet finished. There is more to discover, more to be done. Our earthly life is great and valuable, because there is so much still to be found, still to be achieved. The future offers hard work and great aims. Prester John is the hero of what is still to be done. Thomas still finds a holy place, because his holy finger points to what is not yet achieved. Individual people may hesitate before the great question of reincarnation. They may even ask themselves whether or not they wish to return. But the answer does not lie with them and their preferences. Out of the Heavens the answer descends. The kingdom of Logres is still not established: the Holy Grail is still coming: and hidden in the mysteries of Prester John is the great purpose of Mankind on Earth, towards which Thomas still points.

The true greatness of Mankind is hidden within the Heavens themselves. The coming of Christ from the Heavens to Earth, is the answer to the ancient question: who and what is Man? The knights of King Arthur learnt at the Round Table to perceive what they should expect of themselves. The knights of the Grail discovered powers that were within themselves, although few were yet able to use them. In the Kingdom of Prester John, the apostle Thomas still stretches out his finger and asks who is Christ: what he brought into Man's world on Earth? The answer is still in the Heavens and human souls on Earth have still to follow the pointing finger towards the answer. The future of Mankind lies in what has not yet been done, in the unanswered question, in the great efforts that lie ahead.

Chapter 7

Francisco D'Almeida and the Cape of Africa

Rachael Shepherd

1 The Battle of Granada

On the first of March 1510 there took place a ritualistic death at the mouth of the Salt River on the shores of Table Bay, then called Saldanha Bay, which was perhaps unique of its kind on African soil. It was the death of Francisco D'Almeida which one can read about in history books but where his death is usually attributed to the Hottentots.

Documentary history tells us little about Francisco D'Almeida but we do know that he was born in Lisbon in about 1450 of a noble and wealthy family, and that in the course of life he married and had at least one child.

Quite early in life he joined the Order of Knights of St Iago of Compostela, and was highly regarded in this Order. As a young man he entered into intimate service with the King of Spain, Ferdinand the Catholic, and remained closely connected to him and to his wife, Isabella. He also entered into intimate service with Emmanuel, King of Portugal. Yet earlier, as Ambassador of King Alphonso V of Portugal, he was instrumental in trying to bring about a marriage between Alphonso and Juana of Spain, but this did not succeed. With Alphonso he also went in search of an alliance between Portugal and Louis XI of France. This was likewise in vain, and in witnessing the unfortunate bargaining around the hand of Juana he had been so deeply stirred by the awful way she was treated that he felt the time must soon come when the destinies of nations would no longer be arranged through marriages but by brave and conscious deeds significant for all men.

Finally D'Almeida allied himself to the King of Portugal and in 1492 in his service and as a Knight of the Order of St Iago of Compostela he came to fight with Spain against the Moors at the Battle of Granada. At this battle the Moors were defeated and Spain relieved of their long rule.

In the siege and conquest of Granada which was the last stronghold of the Arabians in Europe the Christian struggle with them reached its height. To reach Granada, the army of Christian knights crossed the snow-covered peaks of the Sierra Nevada. Their plan of campaign had been drawn up by Portuguese and Spanish knights of the Order of St Iago who knew their campaign could have far-reaching consequences. It was a long siege but surrender came at last and the flags of both Ferdinand and the Order were raised. The ensign of the Order planted at Granada contained a sword but in place of the handle was a heart. It was an expression of the intention of the Order that in future the sword must be replaced by love. It was a victory made possible through the good organisation of the Order, and Francisco D'Almeida was among the foremost in the endeavour.

In this battle D'Almeida, then about 42, was badly wounded and would have been killed except that he was taken into their camp by an influential Moorish family, his enemy. This Prince of Arabia was so impressed at the sight of the knight that he begged to have him, and with one of his wives nursed him personally. A real friendship of the heart arose between them and the woman especially cared for him with great love. The deep connection which developed between them led in the course of time to the initiation of Francisco D'Almeida into the mysteries of the writings of Aristotle.

The Moors who had held Granada were in possession of the last work of Aristotle, a priceless and holy book, which had made its way via Alexander the Great through the East before being brought by the Moors to Europe. It is said that this work, called Sierra Nevada, treated of man, the earth and the cosmos. It contained the alchemy of Aristotle and was the last esoteric work of his to reach the West. As he grew better D'Almeida escaped with it and journeyed home. Together with it however he had received a very special alchemistic stone, a pearl, with which a hidden knowledge was associated. This pearl he later wore in a hollow cross around his neck that had been made by a very special goldsmith.

According to the vow he had taken it would have been expected that D'Almeida hand over the book and treasure to the Order of St Iago of Compostela. They considered this to be his duty and their right — also of disposal — since such a work could in any case hardly be appropriated by an individual. D'Almeida however insisted on his right to keep it for himself and also to dispose of it according to his own insight. It was on this basis that he shared its contents with certain others whom he considered rightful persons.

It is alleged that one of these was Thomas Mallory who in quite young years was Archbishop of the Order of St Iago of Compostela. Mallory later returned to England transformed by what he had heard from D'Almeida and created the Morte D'Arthur. This work, especially in the seventh book, can be regarded as the expression in another form of the content of this work of Aristotle.

Mallory also wrote about it more directly. In the book of history which he wrote under the Plantagenet King Henry VII (1485–1508) he describes how he arrived at St Iago of Compostela under danger of his life and there met the Knight Francisco D'Almeida. This man, he said, was the source of all his alchemistic knowledge except for the seventh book of Basilius Valentinus.

Another person unto whom D'Almeida passed on the knowledge and the relic was in fact Stefan Rauter, or Basilius Valentinus as he was known, a man from Alsace, with whom he was intimately connected and who was one of the most famous alchemists of all time. What Valentinus took up from D'Almeida can be found transformed in the seventh of his so-called keys. The seventh key is as follows ...

> Spring, summer and autumn,
> Winter, water and the white salt
> Produce through the light of the sun
> Our work and the admixture.

> Provided that you in weight
> Use not too much nor too little
> Because then it would surely happen
> That your work will not succeed.

> Also seal the glass
> With the hermetic seal
> So that the material
> Will not be eaten by the winds.

In this history of Alchemy, Basilius Valentinus had a very important part to play. Alchemy had been founded as an art by Hermes Trismegistos who also founded the Egyptian civilisation. It was taken further by Maria Hebraica, the sister of Moses, and then by Jews, Persians and Arabs inspired through Alexander by Aristotle until it reached a particular expression in the doctor and philosopher, Avicenna. In the thirteenth Century it began to be Christianised by Thomas Aquinas, Albertus Magnus and Raimundus Lullus until in the fifteenth and sixteenth centuries it in a sense took on a more medical aspect through the persons of Basilius Valentinus and Paracelsus.

Basilius Valentinus himself was born in Mayence. He was a Benedictine and became Prior of the Abbey of Erfurt in 1414. He is said to have had a tremendous knowledge and to have written many books on science, but also to have been the first to extract antimony from sulpharet, though not the first to discover it. He experimented medically with antimony on his fellow monks, sometimes with violent results. He wrote "The Triumph Chariot of Antimony" in which every word has significance. Valentinus was deeply connected with the circle indicated in the story of the Faithful Gerhard and which appeared outwardly as the Bohemian Brothers. An important centre of theirs was Cologne where Albertus Magnus and Thomas Acquinas had also worked. His writings were preserved by his pupils in the Rosicrucian schools of Alchemy and circulated in manuscript form until they were eventually collected and published by Tholde, a secretary of the Rosicrucian Order.

Tholde in his collection includes a few handwritten biographical remarks by Valentinus himself who says it was in peril of his life that he journeyed to St. Iago of Compostela and that those who benefit from the knowledge he brought back should thank God he was able to complete his arduous journey.

Valentinus's work is essentially a study of certain transmutations of carbon, "Coal" or Prima Materia as it is alternatively called. This, the great subject and secret of alchemy, however, he does not reveal. He only hints at it in a somewhat jocular way just as Mallory, who became his pupil when he went to England, hints at it in the story of the Knight Beaumains. Valentinus speaks of a stone that goes through many colours whereas Mallory speaks of it as the Knight with the many coloured armour. The whole of the seventh book of Mallory's "Morte d'Arthur" really shows him as a pupil of Basilius Valentinus.

Carbon is contained in every living substance. It builds the human body and there it takes on all colours in that all organs are made up of its compounds. When it is permeated by soul and spirit it becomes the Philosophers' Stone which is no less than the human being; it is man then who therefore consists of three substances though he is one in essence.

Valentinus described the Philosophers' Stone as being red and white and only discoverable through much prayer, confession and doing good works. It is also possible in the space of three days and three nights to extract the spirit and soul from the physical body. When the human being experiences such a transmutation of body, soul and spirit his ordinary consciousness becomes consciously clair-voyant, i.e. he can see into the spiritual world. This is carbon chem-istry and the content of Valentinus's alchemy. It is described in the fourth key.

> All flesh that came into the world
> Took its origin from the earth.
> It must again become earth,
> And consequently also ashes.
>
> A salt will come from the earth
> That causes the flesh to ensue:
> Which in the mentioned manner
> Is resolved with greatest zeal.
>
> If you desired politely
> To see the form again,
> Then give to the salt
> The sulphur and the mercury.

This hidden knowledge was preserved henceforth in the Rosicru-cian Schools of Alchemy. It goes back to the time of Alexander the Great who learned the secret of substance and its medical use from his teacher Aristotle.

2   Viceroy of India

D'Almeida was placed in command of the Portuguese Navy in 1505 when he was appointed by Emmanuel I as the first Viceroy of India to establish Portuguese authority along the Eastern Coast of Africa and the Malabar Coast of India. In 1505 he captured Kilwa and Mombasa, the latter with great violence and bloodshed. He con-structed forts on the Malabar coast, established his headquarters at

Cochin and introduced the administrative system still in use today. Da Gama had discovered India, D'Almeida conquered it and Alberquergne made it into a lasting Portuguese possession. After having prepared he sailed from Lisbon on 25th March 1507 to take up his post with ships and men financed and commanded by himself. He is said to have been extremely rich and so he could pay for the twenty-two ships and fifteen-hundred fighting men he took with him. Eleven of these ships stayed in India and eleven returned with merchandise. D'Alemida thus became in 1507 the third famous man to round the Cape following Diaz in 1488 and Vasco da Gama in 1497. On his journey to India he wore the gold cross with the pearl inside.

Emmanuel of Portugal had actually planned an attempt to take the Holy Land from the Red Sea and had chosen D'Almeida to carry this out. The purpose was to fall on the back of Islam and so prevent it from entering the heart of Europe. This actually happened but it was part of a five-year plan.

In the State Library in Munich there is a manuscript account of the journey by a German who accompanied the Portuguese to India. People from nearly all European nations were present on this journey because it was inspired by the great chivalric orders, all of which were cosmopolitan and intimately connected above all with the Order of the Knights of St. Iago of Compostela.

D'Almeida soon returned from the first journey and during his stay in Europe handed the book of Aristotle and the reliquary to a woman who in turn gave it to Basilius Valentinus on the hill of Odile in Alsace. This woman was killed soon after by the Order of St. Iago in the Church of Andlau on the Odile Hill because, it is said, of being an accomplice of D'Almeida.

He meanwhile escaped death for the time being as he was again on his way to India, not merely to continue being Viceroy, but to put into action Emmanual's plan of opposing actively from the East the spread of Islam. It had already been repelled from the West at the Battle of Granada. Now it had to be repelled from the East via Africa and the Red Sea, and the Christians even hoped to be able to take Jerusalem from there rather than from Europe.

On his return from India D'Almeida had to encounter at Diu, off the West Coast of India, the combined entire forces of the Arabs and the Sultan of Egypt. It was a formidable fleet for his nineteen ships to face but he won decisively and thus dealt a considerable blow to Islam. In the battle however he lost his son, Lourenco. This was one of the most decisive battles of Asian history. For a hundred years thereafter Portugal had complete supremacy over the Indian Ocean, not politically but as crusader and converter.

It was at this point that those who thought the secret he received at Granada should have been kept within the Order brought about at his recall. He left on 19th November 1509. It was predicted by the witches of Cochin that on his return journey to Europe he would get no further than the Cape of Africa. To this point however he had fair weather, and when he reached Saldanha Bay safely in March 1510 there was tremendous rejoicing, he himself reputedly saying, "Now God be praised; the witches of Cochin are liars who said we should not pass this Cape."

In the "Records of South-Eastern Africa" by Manuel de Faria E. Sousa, Volume 1, it says:

"Near there he put into the bay of Saldanha to take water; and some men going to exchange goods with the blacks, a servant of the Viceroy treated two of them so ill, that they knocked out his teeth and sent him away bloody. Some gentlemen, looking upon this as an affront persuaded the Viceroy to go ashore, when they ought to have advised him to punish his servant for abusing people when they sought relief. This would have been just. He yielded, but so much against his will that as he went into the boat he said, "Ah, whither and to what end do they now carry the sixty years?" hereby declaring that it was an action of rawheads.

There went with him one hundred and fifty, the flower of the ships. They went on to a miserable village, and returned with some cattle and children, when one hundred and seventy blacks coming down from the mountain, whither they had fled, attacked them in defence of their children, casting stakes with sharp points hardened at the fire, so furiously that in a little time they killed fifty gentlemen, and among them the Viceroy, who died kneeling on the sand, with his eyes lifted up to heaven, struck through the throat with one of these stakes. George de Mello returned with the wounded men to the ships, and when he thought the blacks were withdrawn, went ashore and buried the Viceroy and the rest. This was a manifest judgement of God, that so few unarmed barbarians should overcome those who had done such noble actions in India. George de Mello carried the news to Lisbon, where it was received with great grief."

What happened outwardly and through the Hottentots was merely a facade. In reality he had been killed by his own people because of his handling of the book and the pearl. He was killed by an unknown hand with a lance of unusual structure that was driven into his face above the teeth. The lance was of steel and had a peculiar wavy form. Just this unusual form makes the incident inconsistent with the first account by the chronicler Osorius which says he was killed by natives. It was an execution, and those responsible were avenging the betrayal of a secret. They only did not know that a new world order was approaching that made necessary the transmission of certain sources of knowledge to the North. On the tombsone were written the words, "Here rests Francisco D'Almeida who never lied or feared." The tombstone and the tomb were later removed by an unknown hand.

3 The Life of Francisco D'Almeida as Consummation of a More Ancient Past

In the ninth century, Hugo of Tours (800–820) lived a long time on the hill of Odile in Alsace where the mysterious lady who handed over the book of Aristotle to Basilius Valentinus later died. Hugo went to Constantinople for Charlemagne to fetch important Christian reliquaries that were later brought to Rome by Hugo's brother following a vision he had. He brought it to the Church built over the place of Peter's crucifixion. This was a wooden building until the time of Bramante who then built the Templieto there of stone.

In the building of the Templieto, D'Almeida also had a significant hand. The grandson of Ferdinand and Isabella and son of Arthur and Catherine their daughter, the later King Charles, was as a child on the point of dying when he was healed by a wonder. This wonder happened through an appearance of Peter. In acknowledgement of this Ferdinand commissioned the Templieto to be built on the Janiculus in Rome by Bramante. It was the first round church ever to be built and it became the archetype for St. Peters. It was D'Almeida who as ambassador of Ferdinand and Isabella negotiated the permission for this from Alexander Borgia and who also handed Bramante the money for the building.

Later Godfrey of Bouillon, who swore when severely wounded that if he recovered he would fight the Crusade, became the initiator of the Crusades and the co-founder of the Temple order. He reorientated the pilgrimages which had arisen to the grave of Peter in Rome, and for which Hugo of Tours had been responsible through bringing the relic of Peter there, to the grave of Christ in Jerusalem.

Nearchus of Crete was Admiral of the fleet of Alexander the Great and his close friend. Alexander sent him on voyages of discovery in which he circumnavigated the coasts from the Indus to the Tigris and from Arabia to the Gulf of Suez. Alexander even asked him to sail from the East to the Mediterranean in the West by way of the Cape of Africa. He was suppsedly the author of a trustworthy chronicle written before 312 BC that was not so much a history of Alexander as an account of India and his voyage there. This was used later by Strabo, the Greek, the first geographer to describe the Earth, and Arrian who reproduced Nearchus's account. Nearchus was probably killed at Gaza in 312 BC.

Alexander died just as Nearchus came to tell him that the fleet lay ready in the harbour at Babylon to sail around Arabia. Through Alexander's death the journey could no longer take place and so Arabia was not Hellenised. When D'Almeida sailed to India he knew he was sailing the same sea-journey only in the opposite direction on which Nearchus was once about to set out. Behind his voyage to India lay a renewal of the world-embracing ideas of Alexander. They came through D'Almeida from a spiritual community whose esoteric life was founded on the rediscovered alchemy of Aristotle.

In the letters of D'Almeida to King Emmanuel written by Pereira his secretary to which he also put his own rough signature he justifies the measures he has taken comparing them with Nearchus. He says, "In the time of Alexander the interior of the country had to be occupied; we however, must be content with fortifying certain points along the coast thus securing the ocean path to India, for we must now wrest the trade from the hands of the Arabs and take their place." This letter shows for the first time the significance of the ocean route to India.

In the time of Alexander the encompassing of the earth remained to a large degree in the realm of spiritual intention. In the time of the great discoveries it happened particularly in a political and military sense. In our time there is a strong wish to do it in a peaceful and economic way.

Francisco D'Almeida received from the Moor in the form of the book of Aristotle, knowledge about natural and cosmic wisdom. This had passed down from Plato via Aristotle to Alexander, and had made its way first over Asia Minor and Arabia and eventually to Spain. Through this happening the streams of Aristotle and Plato that had previously flowed apart began for the first time to reunite themselves in the West.

D'Almeida was a man who knew of the mysteries of the Hierarchies, of the Grail, of the relationship of nature, God and man, and of the mysteries of the East and the West. One of the reasons he fought the Arabs was that they denied the existence of the hierarchies and tried to wipe this knowledge out. He wanted mankind to know that the spiritual world exists.

If one tries to draw together the threads of his life one can say he began by attempting to establish the alliances of nations through marriages and other means but saw through this experience that they must begin to be created in a new way through individual human consciousness.

He was at the forefrunt of the final victory over the Moors in

Europe and yet found possibly the most significant relationship of his life just with a Moor. Through their bond, the seemingly greatest work of Aristotle came into European hands, and became a seed for a new future.

He was prompted to stand against his Order even to break an old vow, and take upon himself the responsibility for the further distribution of this knowledge. To take such a stand is one of the most difficult things a human being could ever be called upon to do and can only be born out of a tremendous sense of honesty and conviction. He entrusted it to one who gave it artistic form in the Morte D'Arthur, and to another who gave it scientific expression and a further unfolding within the mainstream of European alchemy. He united it thereby with Rosicrucianism whose fountain of knowledge it became. It was thus a deed for both the Arts and the Sciences.

In his own destiny it was received at the threshold of his journey to India. Indeed it seemed to open the door to this journey. How differently did he experience this journey because of it? Did he leave something of its content behind in India and in the East? In his combat of Islam in the East he was as decisive as he had been in the West. And above all it was a cosmopolitan, not just a Portuguese endeavour. The Portuguese had the knowledge and they offered it now that this might be achieved.

Dr W. Zeylmans van Emmichoven, the celebrated Dutch psychiatrist who died in Cape Town in 1961, described Table Mountain as "The altar upon which rests the foot of the World-Cross." D'Almeida felt deeply connected with the story of the Grail. One of the most intimate moments in the Grail story of Wolfram von Eschenbach is a kind of Pieta moment where the dead Schionatulander lies across the lap of Sigune. This scene one could place at the foot of the World-Cross and behold it like the Monk Trevrizent who received them in their flight. So too the ancient experience of the quest for the remains of Peter, the one who denied but who became the great believer, the rock on which the Church was founded. Does the Cape not also have something of the rock on which the Christian world stands? Nearchus, having experienced India, prepared to sail round the Cape of Africa.

D'Almeida had to find the way round Africa in order to reach India. Nearchus had been a part of Alexander's intent to Hellenise the West. D'Almeida's intent was to Christianise the East.

This journey was further very significant because by journeying to India in this way he had to penetrate and journey through the South, an experience Nearchus never had and that was still almost entirely new to northern men. To cross the threshold between North and South was one of the most significant steps in the world. Through D'Almeida the great knowledge of the North, of Aristotle, began its movement to the South, and other knowledge began to move in reverse from South to North.

4   The Cape of Africa

One may seriously wonder why Francisco D'Almeida died so far from Portugal and just at the Cape of Africa. If we consider that when a person of significance dies it is both of importance for the place and of importance for his own future, we may the more ask, why here?

Perhaps some light may be thrown on this by setting it against the background of the events of the time at the Cape. It was first rounded in 1488 by Bartholomew Diaz. Until then it had been called the Cape of Storms but now it was renamed by John of Portugal the Cape of Good Hope. The next person to round it was Vasco da Gama in 1497, and the third was Antonio da Saldanha in 1503. He gave his name to the Bay, calling it the watering place of Saldanha and he was the first to climb the mountain which he also named. D'Almeida was actually the next, but possibly the most inspired description is left to us by Sir Francis Drake who rounded the Cape in the Golden Hind in 1580 on his circumnavigation of the world and described it as "a most stately thing and the fairest cape in the whole circumference of the earth."

The one who lets us glimpse behind the scenes of earthly things however is the Portuguese poet, Camoens in his "Luciads" where he describes the experience of Vasco da Gama as he rounds the Cape and the implications this holds for the future. Da Gama meets a Being who is described by Camoens as follows :

"It was of fantastic form and size and powerful build, with a heavy jowl, unkept beard, and sunken eyes. Its expression was evil and terrifying, its complexion of an earthly pallor. Yellow teeth showed in its cavernous mouth, and its crisp hair was matted with clay. From the size of its limbs it might have passed for a second Colossus of Rhodes, that was one of the seven wonders of the world.

"And then it spoke, in a mighty, terrifying voice that seemed to come from the depths of the sea. Our flesh went creepy and our hair stood on end as we looked and listened.

" 'So, you daring race,' it said, 'bolder in enterprise than any the world has yet seen, tireless in the waging of cruel wars as in the pursuit of hopeless undertakings. So you have crossed the forbidden portals and presumed to sail on these seas of mine, that I have held and guarded for so long against all comers, whether of these regions or any other. You have come to surprise the hidden secrets of nature and of its watery element, that to no mortal, however great, however noble or immortal his deserts, have yet been revealed.

"Listen now to me and learn what perils have been laid up against such excess of presumption, what penalties await you over the vast expanse of ocean and on the land that you will eventually subdue in battle. Know that as many ships as are bold to make this voyage that you are making now will be assailed when they reach this spot by hostile winds and raging tempests; and that on the very first fleet to follow you into these untamed waters I shall wreak such sudden chastisement as to make the danger pale before the reality.

"Here, unless I am deceived, I count on avenging myself to the full on him who discovered me. Nor will the havoc to be visited on your too trusting pertinacity end with this, for every year if my judgement fail me not, your vessels will suffer shipwreck and catastrophe of every sort, until death shall come to seem the lesser evil.

"In these waters that illustrious leader whom fame and fortune are to exalt to the skies as first Viceroy shall meet his end, for so God in his inscrutable wisdom has decreed: here he shall lay down the

100

trophies of his victory over the Turkish fleet. Nor shall the vengeance be mine alone, for his destruction of Kilwa and Mombassa will likewise cry out for retribution ...

" 'Who are you,' I asked, 'for proportions so outrageous take one's breath away?' It rolled its black eyes, contorted its mouth, and, uttering a giant roar that filled me with terror, replied in a voice heavy with bitterness as though the question were one it would gladly have avoided: 'I am the mighty hidden Cape, called by you Portuguese the Cape of Storms, that neither Ptolemy, Pomponius, Strabo, Pliny nor any other of past times ever had knowledge of. This promontory of mine, jutting out towards the South Pole, marks the southern extremity of Africa. Until now it has remained unknown; one of the giant sons of earth, brother to Enceladus, Briareus and the others. With them I took part in the war against Jupiter, as sea captain, disputing with Neptune's squadrons the command of the deep.

It was for love of Thetis, Peleus's wife, that I joined in the campaign. But there was no hope of winning her affection with features as huge and ugly as mine so I made up my mind to have her by force.'"

Later in his poem, Camoens describes D'Almeida in his battle as Viceroy against the Moslems. It is a quite unique description of him, spoken by a nymph :

"But here," she continued her song, "comes another, Francisco D'Almeida, bearing the title of Viceroy and accompanied by his son. He will win for himself as great fame on the ocean as any Roman of old ever did. Father and son together will inflict severe chastisement on Kilwa, expelling the treacherous tyrant who rules over it and setting up a loyal and humane king in his place. Mombassa, a city of fine houses and splendid buildings, they will raze to the ground, destroying all its beauty, in punishment for previous misdeeds.

"On reaching the coast of India, the son Lourenco will himself perform wonders with his ships against the swarming enemy and his artifices. Even though the sea be black with the Samorin's great vessels, the thunderous fire of his guns will put them out of action, smashing rudders, masts and sails to pieces. Then, making boldly for the enemy flagship, he will grapple it fast, leap on board, and account for some four hundred Moslems with sword and lance alone.

"At last, in the inscrutable providence of God, that alone can know the wisdom of its measures, Lourenco will find himself in a position where neither courage nor prudence may avail him. For in Chaul, in a fight with the combined fleets of Egypt and Cambay, a fight so bloody and stubborn that it churns the waters, he will lose his life. Only sheer might can prevail against heroic valour, and here the strength of the swarming enemy, a lull in the wind, and the mounting perils of the sea wil all be ranged against him.

"Could the heroes of antiquity come back to life, what a lesson in courage and nobility might they not learn from the sight of this second Scaeva who can be cut to pieces but not made to surrender. With the whole of one thigh carried away by a chance cannon ball, he still fights on with arms undaunted and a heart as stout as iron. At length another shot snaps the links that hold body and soul together, and his soul, taking wing, will leave its earthly prison behind and soar victoriously aloft.

"Go in peace: after the turbulence of war you have earned tranquil repose. As for your mutilated body, your father is already preparing vengeance. Already I can hear the rolling thunder of his guns and blunderbusses as they dispatch the fierce Cambayans and Mamelukes to the nether regions. Here he comes, stupendous in resolve, blind to everything but grief and lust for revenge, his heart on fire and his eyes tear-drenched with a father's love, confident in his noble rage that he will make the enemy vessels run knee-deep with blood. What he has in mind to do will be seen on the Indus, it will be heard on the Ganges and felt on the Nile.

"Like a jealous bull making trial of its strength for the grim combat ahead, testing his horns against lofty oak or beech and emitting percing roars the while, so Dom Francisco will not descend in fury on the Gulf of Cambay until he has first sharpened his sword on the opulent city of Dabul, humbling its presumptuous daring to the dust.

"From there he will sail to the Bay of Diu, already the scene of famous battles and sieges, and scatter a large if indifferently armed fleet from Calicut that will pin its faith chiefly to its oars. The cautious Egyptian squadron under Malik Yaz will be caught in a hail of cannon-fire and sent to the bottom; while the Cambayan vessels of Nir Husayn, forced by his grapnels to await the avenging wrath of the Portuguese, will see arms and legs tossed on the waves with no bodies to claim them. The victors strike, in their blind fury, like bolts of thunder, and soon there is nothing to be seen or heard save smoke and flames and cries and flashing swords.

"But look: embarking for his native Tagus after his notable triumph, D'Almeida will come near to losing fame and glory through the mournful and ill-fated event I see looming ahead. The Cape of Storms, that is destined to preserve his memory with his bones, will not hesitate to rob the world of so brave a spirit, something that all the might of Egypt and India could not do. Savage Kaffirs, armed only with rude, fire-hardened clubs, will succeed where experienced enemies failed, for all their bows and cannon. The judgements of God are baffling to man. The superstitious, unable to understand them, talk of ill-luck and black misfortune: the workings of Divine Providence are the true explanation."

So why did D'Almeida die at the Cape of Africa? Perhaps at least a part of the answer to this lies in the words of Adamastor. He who crosses forbidden portals has a penalty to pay, a penalty that can be no less a one than death. Da Gama was seemingly the first to be aware of crossing the forbidden portal of the Cape but in D'Almeida this experience was combined with a crossing of forbidden portals in other spheres. For this he had to personally pay a price, but it is as though he also paid the price for daring on behalf of all men who crossed new frontiers in the Age of Discovery.

So the Cape stood as a symbol for the crossing of new and forbidden thresholds. Is not this perhaps a reason why the eyes of the world are upon it also today?

REFERENCES:

- Camoens, "The Lusiads" 1572.
- Manuel de Faria e Sousa, "Records of Eastern Africa" Vol I - John de Barros 1552.
- W.J. Stein, "Portugal as Preparer for the British Mission" - Present Age 1936.
- Encyclopedia Britannica.

Africa, The Heart of The World

J. Lawrence V. Adler

Preface

In trying to look at various aspects of the complicated puzzle that Africa presents to the world, the writer has attempted to use some of the methods of Anthroposophy, the science which seeks to find the living architecture, i.e. the interplay of the spiritual forces underlying and becoming manifest in the phenomena of the world. If it is possible to discover some of the spiritual workings producing the external events of our troubled continent, these may point out the direction where to look for solutions. It is the aim of this article to try and shed some light on the tasks facing the peoples of our continent together with the rest of the world if the serious challenge our dear Africa presents to the healthy development of mankind is to be met constructively.

Men are spiritual beings. Each needs to bring his unique contribution towards mankind's higher development in order to manifest his innate human dignity, no matter what his nationality, race, colour or religion may be. Thank goodness men are not all alike! How boring the symphony of mankind would be, if every member of the orchestra played the same voice, all on the same kind of instrument and in the same key! We must try to discover our individual voices, our different instruments, our different TALENTS so as to worthily perform in the Symphony of Man. This article is addressed to all who feel concerned with the interrelationship between Africa and the rest — especially the Western World — and its implications with regard to world harmony. At times it will be necessary to define certain terms used in Anthroposophy.

The Heart as a Mediator Between the Polarities of the Life and the Death Forces

It has often been stated that man as a microcosm is an image of the world. Thus if one strives to understand the architecture of the world, it is sometimes easier to direct one's first look into what is nearest at hand: the human body. We know its structure and organs in broad outline. Examining their interrelationships and functions may offer insights whose analogies may help us to understand a little of the spiritual workings of the world.

Let us begin by looking at the human heart. How can one somehow characterise it, its function and its position in relation to the geography of the body? One has, however, always to keep in mind that there are no absolute correspondences in nature, but only "tendencies towards a form." As a rule a curve represents what would in the abstract be a straight line.

The world is full of polarities, so is the body. If there is no interspersing medium between polarities, they will either clash — that is, come into cataclysmic contact — or if effectively separated by an inactive, neutral medium, they will remain inert and nothing will

happen. If a connecting medium is interspersed between the extremes, instead of opposing, they now become complements in a process where the tension between them is resolved into a 'conversation', an interchange between them. So it is in the human body.

The head with its senses and the whole nerve system can be regarded as man's pole of perception. In order to function properly it requires peace and quiet. The limbs represent the opposite pole. They, with their muscles, together with the whole metabolic system constitute the opposite pole, of physical movement, of action.

To balance this "conversation" so that it is transformed into creative interplay — that is the function of the heart. However, in order to perform this balancing out, the heart has to perceive the needs, reactions etc. of the periphery, thus it follows that in this respect the heart is a sense organ.

In his "Foundation Stone Meditation"[1] Rudolf Steiner devotes the second of its four parts to the working of Christ. It contains the exhortation: "Übe Geist-Besinnen" (in English, "Practise Spirit-Mindfulness," or "Spirit-Sensing"). In other words: practise endowing your soul with the attribute of "sensing the working of the Spirit" everywhere. This is the heart function in the sphere of human relations i.e. in the social field. The medical profession must learn to recognise how the underlying spirit manifests in polar opposites in different ways. Let us look at this fundamental aspect of any living body. It is, as it were, suspended between two opposing forces. The one comprises the realm of cell formation. Cells "left to their own devices" such as mycelia, yeast or algae, replicate by a process of division, forming virtually endless chains. The direction of growth is centrifugal, and the agglomerate, or lump of chains, swells outwards. As cells form the building blocks of all organisms, we may be justified to name this end of the polarity of life: The Swelling Life-Forces.

The counterpart of these swelling life-forces is its antithesis, that group of modelling, structuring forces which inhibit unbridled, random cell growth. It superimposes upon it the "blueprint" of the body's architecture, compelling the different groups of cells to move away from their own basic patterns; separating and specialising them,

*Trains of swirling vortices
arise when a solid object such
as a stick is drawn through a
stationary liquid, revealing the
formative forces underlying
nature.*

Theodor Schwenk. *Sensitive Chaos,*
(1965). Rudolf Steiner Press, London.
From a photo by the author.

to form the different organs of the body. The action of this group of forces can be likened to pruning. They work from the outside inward, i.e. centripetally. This holds them back, shrinks them, works against them and re-forms them. It is part of that process which is the antithesis of life, the death-forces. Thus we may call this opposite polarity the Formative Death-Forces.

All living creatures exist through the grace of a harmonious interplay between these two polarities. The word 'Grace' is used very consciously, for no human intelligence can hope to grasp such an infinity of complex interrelationships. It is nothing else than a tangible expression of the blessing of that being who is the Lord of the Forces of Harmony: the Christ. Christ is the Lord of the divine mediating heart-forces. In the above-mentioned "Foundation Stone Meditation" there appears the sentence, "For the Christ-Will holds sway in the encircling round, blessing the souls."

This becomes very relevant when we examine how the embryonic

heart is formed. The first sign of life in the embryo is the starting of a peripheral circulation of the embryonic fluid. In other words, the whole embryo is the scene of an all-pervading heart process which

Above — Vortices push into the surrounding liquid like the ball part of a joint into its socket. Below — drawing showing the absolute streamlines of the train of vortices revealed in the above illustration.

Theodor Schwenk. *Sensitive Chaos,* (1965). Rudolf Steiner Press, London. Above: from a photo by the author. Below: drawing by Walther Roggenkamp.)

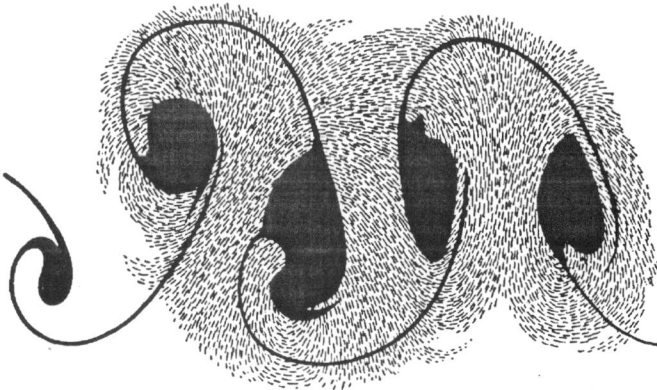

brings the polarities of the swelling life-forces and the formative death-forces into a creative interplay.

The embryonic fluid begins to specialise, some of it forming into blood corpuscles. The structuring effect of this circulation imprints "flow-patterns" in the fluid.[2]   In the 'eddies' these corpuscles aggregate, forming the first blood-vessels, and out of these the first primitive heart forms.   Now the circulation undergoes a complete change. In passing through this heart, it is transformed from a peripherally-orientated, to a heart-centred system. Though the details are only superficially touched upon, one important factor emerges: the heart is formed by, i.e. results from the circulation, it did not initiate it. In the course of this article we shall try to show that the analogy of this, when applied to the world has a far reaching significance.

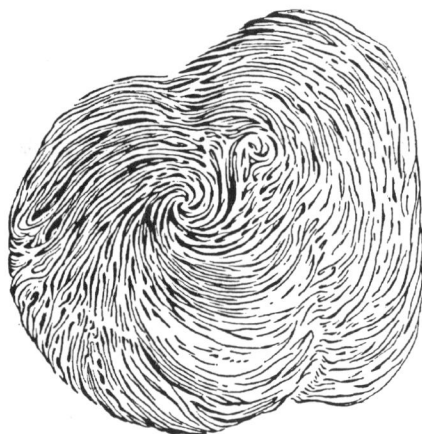

Spiralling fibres at the apex of the heart.

Theodor Schwenk. *Sensitive Chaos,* (1965). Rudolf Steiner Press, London. Drawing by Walther Roggenkamp.)

In the same Christ-orientated part of the meditation cited above, there also appear the lines: "Let there be fired from the East, what from the West is formed." The heart too has an "Eastern" and a "Western" side, which conform to the qualities mentioned in the

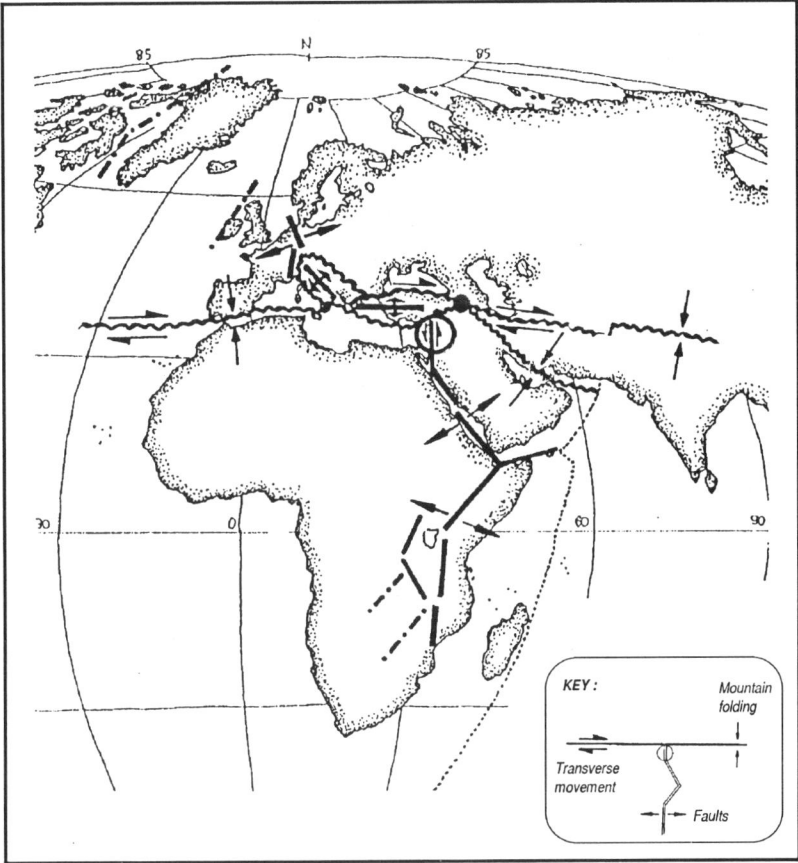

Diagram showing the shape and position of Africa straddled across the Equator; as well as the principal fault and fold lines revealing the underlying geology of the continent.

(After Schmutz, 1988; in *Child and Man* Vol. 29 No. 2. Steiner Schools Fellowship 1995.)

verse. The right, its "Eastern" half contains the warm, fiery, red, arterial blood, full of upbuilding, nutrient (oxygen-rich) solutions; whereas the left "Western" half holds the cooler, blueish, denser, venous blood laden with precipitates, the products of the hardening processes of the body.

The heart has four chambers, divided by two walls, forming a cross. The vertical axis of this cross has approximately the same inclination as has the axis of the earth. Africa "bulges" to the West — the heart's pericardium also bulges a little on its "western" side.

Let us now look at the whole earth, always keeping in mind that there are no absolutes in geography. One must look at tendencies, "gestures" as it were.

Other continents are heart-shaped too, but they are elongated as in South America, truncated (Australia), but most heart-like in the case of Africa, especially if one includes Madagascar and the Arabian Peninsula which form part of the Eastern lobe of Africa and geologically belong to it.

Roughly symetrically situated above and below the equator, almost midway between South America and Australia, Africa occupies a central position in the world and, like the human heart, is flanked by two, roughly equal-sized lungs: the Atlantic and the Indian Oceans. Circulating ocean currents wash the edges of the continents. They too are warm in the East and cold in the West. These western currents are rich in precipitates of the sea, in their fish life.

Such a heart position becomes even more telling, if one comes across yet further analogies between the human body and the earth.

The Human Body and the Earth's Anatomy

Take the Head for instance. As was stated above, the head (together with the nerve-sense organisation) can be regarded as the pole of perception. It is round: the soft brain, harder than the cerebro-spinal fluid, yet not rock hard like the bones, is like "frozen water." Its hard, bony shell, is closed on top, its "northern" end.

Below, in its lower, most "southernly" part is the jaw. There it develops towards a point. It can even move a bit like a limb. The tongue has similar characteristics: in the "North" it is almost immobile, grown fast to the head; in the "South" it becomes pointed and can move. The limb-character of jaw and tongue becomes even more evident through their capacity to work — i.e. to chew and talk.

The polar opposite of the head are the limbs. They are elongated, with hard bones inside and soft flesh, i.e. muscles, surrounding them on the outside. The humerus and the femur have wide, spherical "northern" ends which are nearest to the head and can rotate. Towards their "southern" end they grow thinner and have bifurcated terminations which can only form a hinged joint. This tendency, to be roughly spherical (head-like) above, and to splay out into points away from it becomes progressively more pronounced the further they move away from the head; each limb terminates by dividing up into five pointed digits. The limbs with their muscles, together coupled with the whole metabolic system constitute, as stated, the opposite pole of physical movement, of action.

Here too, the middle chest region which houses the heart, plays a mediating role. To the "north" i.e. on top, the rib-cage is woven together into a skull-like, hard, solid dome, protecting the soft, inner organs. Proceeding downwards, the ribs move apart, hard bone is interspersed with softer tissue, till eventually the ribs, now limb-like, moving with each breath, recede and the soft abdomen takes over.

Now, let us take a look at the geography of the earth. The North Pole consists of a huge mass of floating ice - frozen water, like the gel of the brain, floating on the cerebro-spinal fluid. The Arctic is girdled by islands and the rocky shores of the northern Continents, i.e. a kind of "skull." It too is soft inside, hard outside. The South Pole has a core of land surrounded by oceans — hard inside, soft outside. All the Continents, most of the earth's peninsulas, and many of its major islands have a rounded northern, and a pointed southern profile. The North exhibits head-like, the South limb-like characteristics. Europe has the most peninsulas — land masses interspersed

113

with great seas. In the South they carry on into Asia with its great inland seas: the Black, Caspian and Aral seas, etc. In the West, (interrupted by the North Atlantic Ridge) they cross the Atlantic Ocean and re-emerge as the Great American Lakes and the Hudson Bay. Europe provides a kind of rib-cage, through which the most important East-West winds breathe, interconnecting land and seas.

But what of the contention, implied in the title of this article, that Africa is the heart of the world? We must first do a little more ground work to be clear about some of the intrinsic aspects of a reciprocal relationship.

The Reciprocal Relationship Between the Physical and the Spiritual World

Let us look at the relationship of an architect to his building. While he is busy planning it, his mind is full of it, but there is as yet no physical structure. Once the house is erected and complete, in other words physically there, his inner, spiritual activity stops. He has as it were emptied the content of his mind into the building of brick and mortar and can now move on to fresh fields.

In other words: the Spiritual potential and its physical realisation, or incarnation, stand in an opposing reciprocal relationship and are thus mutually exclusive.

One can schematize this as follows :

Spiritual activity (planning)   —   No physical house
Physical house (standing there) —   No more spiritual activity

   or

Spiritual archetype   —   "Empty Space" on earth
Physical incarnation —   "Empty Space" in the spiritual world

i.e. a reciprocal relationship is one of inverse congruity.

The Reciprocal Relationships In the African Continent

Africa is surrounded by almost uninterrupted coastal mountain chains enclosing a high plateau. Thus in section it resembles a chalice. The floor of this central plateau is scored by two main furrows: The rift valley, the Nile basin running from its northern shore right down into Mozambique. (Its outrunners, continuing right down to the Cape, are brought up short by Table Mountain). This vertical slash is traversed at right angles by Africa's major east-west valley, the Congo Basin. The two form a mighty valley cross.

Thus the "Chalice of Africa" encloses a heart-shaped "Empty Space", quartered by the cross incised into its floor. But we said that a physical empty space corresponds to a spiritual potential or archetype; so *Africa can be said to contain, or circumscribe an empty space "a spiritual heart."*

Rudolf Steiner has called Africa the *Mercury Continent*. What could he have meant by that? The ancients, when they spoke of mercury, meant life-forces; for instance the Mercury Staff symbolises the art of healing. To the alchemists mercury was the quintessential liquid, and liquid is the physical vehicle of the life forces.[3] Africa has practically no mercury and relatively little water. Is this another manifestation of a reciprocal relationship: does it perhaps have spiritual life-forces, spiritual healing-forces, which have not come down to earth, i.e. which have not incarnated? [4]

Gardeners tell us that you can grow almost anything in this country if you have enough water. In other words, there is a great *life-potential*; but it is generally unable to come to realisation in the form of living plants growing on the earth, simply because there is too little life-supporting water.

Africa has the oldest geology of the earth. It stands longest above sea level, its last rejuvenating inundation took place long before the more recent ones of other continents and it is physically hardened, atrophied. Most of Africa's rivers are dry for the greater part of the

115

year. Apart from underground seepage, they do not flow, their barren, sunken beds cracking as the merciless sun scorches all but the deepest rooting plants and trees; their gutted exposed banks torn and gullied by wind and water erosion. These rivers should be the flowing arteries of the life-blood of the earth, feeding her creatures, carrying away her hardening salts. Over aeons, Africa's rivers have become old, functioning erratically, they have indeed become hardened arteries. Water should *weave* in the living sap of stones and plants, the blood of animals and man; and thus literally occupy a median realm between heaven and earth. If, in flood, it burrows too deeply *below* the earth's surface, it becomes destructive and brings death in its wake; if it rises too high into the sky and no longer precipitates as rain, death also follows. In order to sustain life, i.e. in order to be the bearer of the *spiritual* life forces on earth, water must be physically present *between* heaven and earth. If it is absent, the spiritual potential of the life-forces may be ever so great, but they cannot discharge into physical existence and bring about life here on earth.

We tried to show that all mediating, flowing, rhythmicising "water-functions" (in this case the rivers) belong to the realm of the heart forces. Could it be that in calling Africa the Mercury continent, Steiner meant to indicate that Africa is the bearer of the spiritual heart forces, that Africa contains the spiritual, (potential) heart of the earth? In anthroposophical terminology one would call it the *etheric heart of the earth* which however has problems in becoming effective on earth because of the drying up of its physical correlate: water.

The Etheric or Formative Life-forces and the Astral Forces

Before we try to examine some aspects of the *activity* of this spiritual or etheric heart we must clarify a few more concepts.

At the beginning of this article we spoke about the swelling life-forces and the formative death forces and that all life-processes are interactions between these two parameters. So, grouping the above polarity together into one concept, we can call them the *formative*

116

life-forces, or in anthroposophical terminology: *the etheric forces.*

Just as the engineering structure one can speak of a *body* of forces and counterforces peculiar to that structure, so one can call the particular combination of life-forces of an organism its *formative life-forces body*, or for short its *etheric body.*[5]

Feelings were held to originate in the realm of the fixed stars, hence the name Zodiac which means "circle of animals". Each kind of animal and each human being has a different, distinctive constellation of feelings which give it a characteristic stamp. Ancient wisdom considered the animals to be the representatives of the whole realm of feelings. Anthroposophy is able to throw light on the reality of this connection between the life of feelings and the stars. As the word "star" derives from the Greek "Aster", anthroposophy employs the terms the *Astral Forces*, or *Astrality* to designate the forces of feeling.

As above, one can call an animal's or a person's constellation of astral forces his Astral Body[6] Man too has feelings but it is the presence of his *ego that distinguishes him from the animal.* His ego enables him to say, "No" to his instincts and thus enables him to lift himself above their realm.

Reincarnation, Karma and Atlantis

Three more terms need to be defined and clarified before we have a foundation from which to explore further:

Reincarnation :[7] this simply means rebirth. Anthroposophy defines this term as: man being reborn in a human body. Let us try to describe it in a simplified picture: just as in a business organism the various departments have to draw an annual balance sheet and will then start the new year afresh with the *result* of the previous year's work before them, (their credit, or debit balance) so after death man has to "audit", that is digest his life's deeds and draw "up a balance of his credits and debits". This implies putting out of his mind the nitty gritty of his daily experiences in order to arrive at the "net result" of his life his "Profits and Losses". With these he will start his new life, "build up a new business of life" as it were. Without

117

reincarnation man would be irretrievably locked up in his present range of possibilities and could never surpass them i.e. The possibility to reincarnate is the starting point for man's infinite path of development towards his spiritual potential.

The Law of Karma [7] could be described thus: A person has to meet the necessary consequences of his actions by coming into such situations in a later life that his earlier actions' significance for his and his fellows' development may dawn on him and become a spur and a steppingstone for further development.

Atlantis : [8] From Plato, to Steiner, to Credo Vusamazulu Mutwa[9] and since, innumerable authors have written about the ancient continent of Atlantis which was submerged by the deluges of the Ice Age. Plato places it in the vicinity of the Azores. It is interesting that many place names right around the northern Atlantic Basin contain syllables such as "atl" "elt" "tla" etc. which seem to have their root in "Atlantis" : from Mexico's Popocatepetl, Tlaxiaco etc., Africa's Atlas Mountains, right up to Iceland's Kötluangi and Greenland's Qutdligssat etc., to name only a few.

According to Steiner, in Atlantean times all earthly substances were still more fluidic than today, so were men's bodies. Because of this the formative life-forces could work much more immediately into all of creation. By the same token man had more direct access to the formative life-forces and could manipulate them to serve him in a similar way as we today manipulate sub-physical forces: such as electricity, magnetism, nuclear forces, genetic forces etc.

Due to this more fluidic state of earth and nature, man did not incarnate as deeply as today. He was still more "in touch" with the world of the stars, and it penetrated his formative life-forces. In other words, his astral and etheric forces were much more intimately interwoven than today. This gave them immense power, for all his feelings stirred up mighty etheric reactions. Towards the end of the Atlantean time, corruption set in and these powers were abused. Eventually this abuse became so unbridled that the cosmic balance between the etheric and astral forces in nature broke down and floods destroyed the continent. The story of the flood is a description of these events.

Similar stories can be found in almost all mythologies. No mythology could maintain such a story for long periods if it were mere "fabrication". The universal presence of it suggests a foundation of truth, quite apart from the geological evidence. Why do we bring all this here? We spoke of the law of Karma, that man must face the consequences of his actions. Mankind has a Karmic debt to pay for the abuse of its etheric powers in Atlantis. When the inundations took place, people moved away from their "Epicentre" in various directions. Some of the southernmost of these streams moved into Africa, probably via the Congo Basin. (See Credo Mutwa's maps on the frontispiece of his book). Rudolf Steiner has said words to the effect that the Black race carries the impulses of Atlantis into modern times. There is some evidence to support this contention. Consider the very strong instinctive drive-forces in Africa, (and now infiltrating the West). Drives are an interpenetration of subconscious astral and etheric forces and are as such today's correlate of Atlantean conditions.

The automatic patterning, rhythmicising of all artistic expression, (be it dancing, singing, carving, decorating, building or whatever) into endlessly repetitive motifs is a sign that the etheric forces still work instinctively and have not risen into the realm of conscious thought. That is why they on the one hand are so infallibly right; but on the other, why there is no change, no unfolding, no development, no motif metamorphosing to a climax such as for instance in Western music, Nordic art etc. (Whilst it is understood that individuals stand out against the norm, it is a truism that such general traits do exist nevertheless). However tempting, it would transcend the scope of this article to go into further details, this may be done at a later occasion.

We stated that the Black race carries the impulses of Atlantis into modern times. The Black races have carried Atlantean impulses and perpetuated them in Africa, in a way carrying on with them right into modern times. They have borne the Atlantean karma for the whole world for a long time. The time to carry this burden is almost over. Africa's awakening is showing that. They are no longer prepared to be ignored in world events. What actually happened?

Atlantean Karma has been Implanted into Africa

When the Atlantean age drew to a close, the people of Europe embarked upon a period of world-wide migrations. They were given a chance "to start afresh". For a limited time (thousands of years are but a short span in world evolution) they were spared from having to face the consequences of the karmic debt they owed for their abuse of the life-forces in old Atlantis. They went through a period of world-wide migrations, in order to start new civilisations with fresh impulses. For this interim period in world evolution they did not have to pay their karmic debt — not yet. This period of grace, with all the world's development speeding up immeasurably, is now rapidly drawing to a close.

The black races did not participate in the development of their northern brothers. They as it were "held the fort" for mankind, until it would be ready to take up its challenge once more and face its karmic debt with its newly gained powers of consciousness.

If then mankind fails to meet the challenges of its postponed karma out of its own insight and free will, it will have to pay an infinitely higher price, for the laws of karma are inexorable and must be paid when the time is ripe. Atlantean Karma is World Karma, and as such is the concern of all mankind. The problems of Africa are of world significance and are a world challenge.

This article is a preliminary attempt to illuminate some phenomena which seem to support these theses. In the process we shall try to observe where these phenomena point to, if one follows through their gestures. That is, what course of action are they trying to suggest to us so that the impulses of the spiritual world (of which the physical facts are merely symptoms) can begin to work in men's hearts and bring blessing to mankind?

We stated that in Atlantean times all substances and bodies were more fluidic and thus provided a very responsive medium into which the etheric forces could work with great immediacy and power, and that these properties were abused. Today Africa's soil is dry and hard, there is too little water to channel down etheric forces for growth. Apart from its other implications, on the agricultural level this seems to present the following Karmic challenge: (for as stated before, Africa still carries the karmic debt of the world).

Through becoming conscious of this lack of water, man's outer and inner hunger has to lead him to seek those *spiritual insights* by means of which he can, through unegotistical human work, create new conditions for etheric forces to flow and bring blessing to the world, and Africa in particular.

That such a challenge is not just a local African concern seems to be borne out by phenomena such as the world-wide participation in "Operation Hunger." It is a tragedy that this noble impulse was not accompanied by spiritual insight into the deeper issues that needed to be tackled, and so it was bound to abort.

Another indication of such world concern was the work of Richard St. Barbe Baker and his "Men of the Trees." They started the re-afforestation of Kenya and the Sahara. The following citations from his book *My Life, My Trees* [10] give an idea of the spirituality of his outlook. No wonder he had so much success!

Let us look at page 146. "The Sahara Reclamation Programme provides a challenge so arresting that it could unite all the countries who have fought so long for their freedom and liberation from colonialism". On p. 155 he cites the title of a lecture he held in Brisbane: "Sahara Reclamation and How it could Relieve World Tensions". On page 163 he states: "Too often the isolationist and racial attitudes are characteristic of the separatist tendencies against which we of the Men of the Trees ....must make a stand."

This seems to indicate a direction for tackling Africa's (and therewith the world's) problems with a more likely chance of success than all the (now, thank goodness no longer operating) anti-apartheid measures. It must be stated here however, that reverse apartheid still operates in many of Africa's liberated states.

Let us look at apartheid a little more closely.

Apartheid, a Symptom of the Sickness of the World

The chaos wrought in the balance of nature in Atlantean times is imprinted as a schism into Africa's etheric structure, expressing itself in a basic contrast: burning heat and too little water. Water is *the* element in nature which, more than any other, mediates between polarities and brings them into a rhythmical, harmonious relationship.

In this sense it performs a heart function in the realm of physical nature. Its absence means that the mediating substance, water is lacking as the vehicle for resolving the chaos. Apartheid, be it the former South African variety, or be it tribal or national variations, or reverse apartheid (Black against White) or its American variety, or the castes of India, or the Jews in Europe etc., etc.,. is by no means overcome yet. Spiritually, it is an expression of the poverty of heart forces, a spiritual drought.

Thrombosis - preventing the heart forces from flowing and causing a drought of blood — is one of the world's major killer diseases. Is this perhaps a symptom of mankind's clogged heart i.e. its *love* forces? This spiritual drought of heart forces is found all over the world. World Apartheid, be it caste, race, class, politics, religion, nationalism or whatever; that is the real Atlantean inheritance of the world that needs to be addressed. Its most serious manifestation seems to be the East/West conflict which, though no longer expressing itself as Russia *vs* the West, has now substituted China and other communist countries, Mohammedanism and many other "enemies" — i.e. the East/West apartheid is still going strong. The interesting thing was not that apartheid was found elsewhere (lamentable though that may be), but that the world's attention was focused on its South African manifestation. It looked at South Africa with a feeling of hot resentment: the world's heart was not functioning properly. This reminded one of the Nazis projecting their sense of having failed to be "Christian," onto those living examples of a people who had also failed to achieve Christianity — the Jews. They tried to destroy externally what can only be brought about by inner self-change. One might wonder if the

World Council of Churches, as well as those individual churches which supported armed conflict against the then South African government, were not falling into a related trap, however genuine their humanitarian concern for the suffering of the suppressed may have been. Revolution cannot remedy the basic condition, it only drives the illness underground, as in Europe and in most new African states — with disastrous results.

We shall now have to come back to the geographical significance of the South. It is not unimportant to note that in all of Africa its southern tip — South Africa — is on the one hand most deeply penetrated by western consciousness forces, while on the other hand it displayed most crassly its 'heart disease'. It is the general similarity of consciousness of standard Western thinking which simultaneously impressed the West with a feeling of kinship — and revulsion: "South Africa represents that part of me that is mortally sick. I wish I could cut out this festering sore!"

Europe's rich humus of old civilisation seems to bury and hide many of its ills; on the other hand Africa's erosion, its hard impenetrable soil drives them to the surface, naked, for all to see. South Africa was merely the ugly duckling, the unsavoury symptom of the sickness of the whole world.

At the beginning of the article we pointed out that the human heart comes into being through the peripheral circulation. The sicknesses of the body can only be healed if its circulation is put into order. After all, if it could heal itself it would not be sick in the first place. Thus its circulation had to be cured from its periphery inwards if it was to be really effective; it could not be expected to effect a spontaneous cure by itself. So, if the world really wanted to build up its heart forces, if it really wanted to heal the sickness of apartheid as a symptom of its own global pathology, it had to heal some of its own international "apartheid" first.

Mikhail Gorbachev was the first to begin this healing process. The result was spontaneous and immediate. Only a few years later, South African apartheid crumbled and disappeared.

Long before this actually happened, this article prophesied that this was the only way to heal the body of the world of the sickness of apartheid: *peripheral World Apartheid would have to begin to disappear, then the South African variety would soon follow suit.* In other words: it was a matter of healing the head and limbs, then the heart would automatically cure itself. It demonstrates that if the symptoms are read aright, eventually the facts of the world bear out the analysis.

Before going further we need to define two more concepts.

Consciousness-Soul and Spirit-Self

When one studies the development of mankind, one discovers that there are periods of approximately two thousand years during which a certain soul-faculty is acquired. When a new period draws in, mankind will begin to slowly develop a quite different approach to the new problems with which this age confronts it.

For instance, in the Greek age, man had to come to terms with the world, he had to acquire an altogether new faculty to understand the world, he had to understand it more intellectually. The successive philosophical schools came to grips with this problem in an ever more intellectual way until it reached its flower in the scholasticism of the thirteenth century.

With the dawn of the Renaissance, an altogether new attitude began in the history of mankind. Man began to regard the world with a drive to master the world with a clear, conscious understanding of how it really worked. He strove to master it in all the forms of his art. Soon the age of the great discoveries was to begin, followed by all the various new forms of science.

This, the striving to 'creep into,' to so identify with the physical or social phenomena, that it is not I who judge, or speak *about* them, but that they as it were should speak *through me* became his striving. Look at Leonardo's or Dürer's drawings, Raphael's or Rembrandt's portraits, Shakespeare's characters: in each case the artist so effaces himself that the things, the character he depicts, speak for themselves without needing an 'interpreter.' Many socio-historical phenomena indicate that mankind is striving to master this new kind of consciousness. Modern psychology has coined a new term which approaches this concept closely and calls it *Empathy*. This can roughly be defined as, "To feel one's way into the other, to lose one's judgemental attitude and to so objectively submerge oneself into a person's individuality by means of a work of art or whatever, that this identification becomes a new form of perceptual experience, from within the perceived object as it were."

This new attitude Rudolf Steiner calls *the Consciousness-Soul attitude*. The time span favourable for the acquisition of this new faculty he calls the *Consciousness-Soul Age*. Perhaps its character emerges most clearly when questions such as, "What ails thee, my brother?" or "What is it you feel destined to bring to the world?" are asked at the deepest level.

The next developmental epoch which must be prepared for now, though it still lies in the distant future, Rudolf Steiner calls the *Spirit-Self Epoch*. In that his higher being can unite with it here on earth. From a certain point of view one might perhaps call the spirit-self attitude a Christianising of the *Consciousness-Soul attitude,* in that one so intensifies one's participation in the other's (my brother's) sufferings and achievements that they become my own sufferings, my own joy. I know of no more moving expression of the Spirit-Self attitude than the following verse:

> So long as thou dost feel the pain
> Which I am spared,
> The Christ, unrecognised,
> Is working in the world.
> For weak is yet the spirit
> While each is only capable of suffering
> Through his own body.
> — *Rudolf Steiner*

World concern with human suffering does begin to reveal a glimmering, a first flash of this Spirit-Self attitude, but as yet it is often purely intellectual and has so far manifested but very little connection to real life. Why is that so? The world must first fully absolve the Consciousness-Soul stage, to learn to ask genuine questions, instead of proposing all sorts of intellectual "solutions" where no questions were asked, of ready made answers to questions that have not yet arisen, or whose implications have not yet been clearly understood, neither by the sufferer, nor the expert. To ask the right questions, that is the archetypal heart quality, the quality of being silent and letting the other speak out his innermost concerns. That, in a nutshell, is the Consciousness-Soul attitude.

There arises another problem though, the discernment between the other's true *crie de coeur*, his genuine heart's aspirations, and what he says he would like to have; these may be very different things indeed.

Anthroposophy i.e. Spiritual Science and Phenomenology

It is here where anthroposophy, the modern science of the spirit, can help. Steiner defined anthroposophy as "A path of knowledge which would guide the spiritual in the human being to the spiritual in the world."[11] The discipline of anthroposophy entails the study and practise of the spiritual potential in man; the striving to recognise this potential, which may also be called his divine image, and to translate it into a practical realisation on earth. The practise of anthroposophy is the striving along this path, towards realising, of incarnating this image of man here on earth. One of the tools of anthroposophy is the practising of phenomenology, also referred to as *'Goethean Observation.'* This is hinted at in the first paragraph of this article. Phenomenology in the anthroposophical sense, is the art of observing, studying the phenomena of the physical world intensely, until the underlying spiritual principles reveal themselves.[12]

Only when the world manages to develop the Consciousness-Soul attitude of true, phenomenological heart-listening, will it have taken the first step towards illuminating the enigma of dark Africa, towards solving Africa's world-Karma. Only if Africa's people feel spiritually

126

recognised will they be able to unburden their pent up suffering; will Africa's spastic heart forces begin to flow. Only when the world manages to transform its intellectual 'judgemental' attitude towards the problems of Africa and its southern tip, into active involvement of its sacrificial will forces into Spirit-Self qualities, only then will Africa's world-Karma begin to be resolved, will the world's heart begin to form anew and function here on earth.

What does 'active involvement of sacrificial will forces' mean?

The Manicheans (of around the fifth century) said, "You must let the dragon swallow you, so that you can transform him, 'en-Christian' him from within."

Africa needs the leaven of the highest achievement of western European culture: Christian spiritual awareness, that is Christian esoteric science, i.e. anthroposophy, so that it can recognise the world's heart-forming processes and inwardly respond to them.

This does not in the first place mean that Europe should send lecturers, it should not feel called upon to *teach* Africa. The very converse is called for: the sublimation of phenomenology. How can one do this? *By planting spirit impulses into work on the earth,* by applying anthroposophy to practical spheres so that the soil is fertilised with man's work, that it is literally prepared to receive the fruits of man's spiritual striving on earth. Only then will anthroposophy find also a spiritually fruitful soil, in which spiritual seeds have a chance to germinate, because the foundation of the will has been prepared out of which the true spiritual questions will in time sprout. This should not be taken pedantically. These two, the challenge of work, and the challenge of transmitting esoteric learning, do not have to be met in chronological order, they must interweave to form the fabric of the world's heart.

Esoteric simply means the spiritual principles underlying the exoteric (outer, sense perceptible) phenomena of the physical world.

Just as the human heart was formed out of the circulation emanating from the periphery, so the world heart can only be freed from its frozen enchantment, through reviving the circulation of the world's nations' concerns in one another and, inter alia, South Africa. This process has only just begun. May it continue to develop!

The sharing of concern in the other is a very different thing from all other kinds of sharing. When you share goods, you so easily start from a position of strength and self assurance: *I have* and *I give.* This *I have* implies a certain aggressiveness, a threat to the receiver, by the personality of the "rich giver." In its mildest form it expresses itself as paternalism, in its worst form this position of strength becomes bullying, or, on an international level, armed threats and war with all its horrors. As in physics every force has its equal and opposite counterforce, so belligerence must breed reprisal and can never heal. When you share *a concern* you do not start from a strong, "safe" position. Concern does not mean knowing the answers, it is an anxious regard for, a suffering with the other and implies an element of uncertainty, of weakness. *True heart's concern is the interchange of vulnerabilities, of weaknesses and the only safety is* <u>trust</u>. Awareness of peoples human weakness, that is the preparation for understanding Christ's saying, "If two people meet in my name, I am there amongst them." It is this awareness of weakness that creates the space for Christ's strength to work through men's *deeds.* "Not my, but Thy strength; not my, but Thy will flow out of our encounter" — perhaps this is the essence of Christian concern.

Challenges to South Africa

How can one participate in the task of building the world's heart from within South Africa? Today many people suffer in this country. What can the privileged whites do? It was stated that the heart is a sense organ. Then surely we, as inheritors of the West's achievements in consciousness have the task to help in developing Consciousness-Soul and Spirit-Self awareness in ourselves.

Christ's strength is His total empathetic acceptance of weakness and suffering just because man is weak and suffers. His total empatheric joy is brought into being by man's every step towards the unfolding of his higher self — no matter how humble his steps may appear to be.

128

In other words His is a total commitment to man. He does not stand apart, but *with* man — this is an image which can guide one towards Spirit-Self development. Just as the world is challenged to develop heart consciousness, so are we, at the heart of the earth, challenged to develop peripheral, world-embracing consciousness. We are challenged to sense the spirit impulses working from the whole world, to heal the heart.

Let us look once more at the duality of the formative life-forces as part of the fundamental polarity of expansion and contraction. The latter also embraces other sets of opposites: Joy and pain; unconsciousness and consciousness etc.

The one Polarity of Expansion embraces such attributes as: joy; unconsciousness; the swelling life forces. This is experienced every night when, after a hard day's work one blissfully stretches out in bed and sinks into a refreshing sleep.

The other Polarity, Contraction, comprises aspects such as: pain; hardening of the formative forces etc. These are graphically experienced when one is hurt. The sudden drawing in of the breath; tears are squeezed out; the posture collapses; sobbing (exhaling) ensues; acute awareness of pain; the hardening of the scab which prevents further dissipation of blood (i.e. expansion); followed by exhaustion — the ebbing of the life-forces — everyone has experienced this. Think of sayings such as, "Joy builds one up, but pain forms one." Let us summarise these polar opposites :

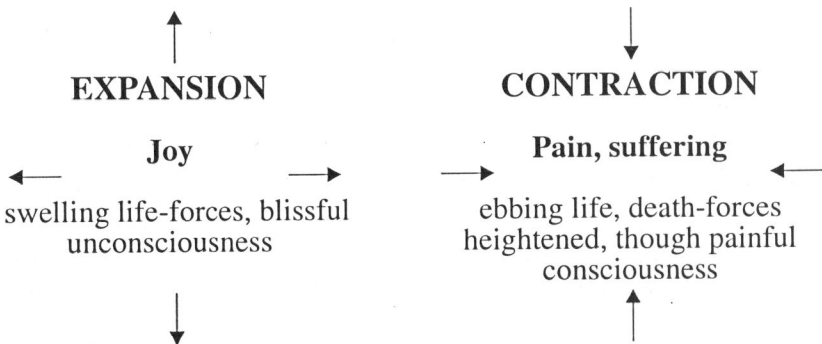

↑	↓
EXPANSION	**CONTRACTION**
Joy	**Pain, suffering**
← →	→ ←
swelling life-forces, blissful unconsciousness	ebbing life, death-forces heightened, though painful consciousness
↓	↑

129

Africa has sparse growth — this is a result of the working of the contractile (pain producing) forces. In nature the formative forces preponderate, their hardening effects limit the swelling life-forces and they experience difficulty in unfolding and proliferating. i.e. Formative forces overrun and inhibit the swelling life forces.

Europe's lush nature displays the preponderance of the swelling life forces over the formative life-forces, (i.e. in a lush, blossoming meadow in Spring).

Africa needs the softening of its too formed out life-forces, its water household must be refreshed by Europe's overabundant water (i.e. life-forces).

Spiritually, European culture is losing its vitality, the drying up of its water-reserves is an expression of its life-forces being squeezed out, stifled by an excess of dead formative-forces, spoiled by technology's inroads into natural ecosystems, causing them to break down under unaccustomed, too heavy strains being placed upon its resources. It needs Africa's inner vitality, not yet spoilt by pollution, to rejuvenate its flagging life-forces, i.e. Europe needs Africa's vitality to seize upon and to stimulate its aging swelling-life-forces.

The swelling-life-forces and the formative-death-forces, though working from opposite directions, need to interpenetrate each other, then they will mutually fructify i.e. stimulate each other to new manifestations of life. Technologically created formative forces cannot play this role; because they are too "chemically pure," they have been created to serve a too narrow function, and do not take the whole ecology into account.

Thus they rob the substances they contact of their innate swelling-life-forces; in order to become more universal. Chemical forces thereby widen their relationship to a broader spectrum of the world, preying upon the swelling-life-forces they encounter. Thus they sate their inbuilt hunger; their imbalance; their chemical appetite upsets the balance of nature in the process. A good example for this type of abuse can be found in artificial fertilizer which robs the soil of fertility. One has to apply ever increasing amounts of fertilizer, until after a number of years a complete or at best partial desertification has taken place. Natural Muck Fertilisation on the other hand improves the land.

Similarly, weakened swelling-life-forces can go on a rampage; robbing adjacent formative-death-forces to restore their own one-sidedness. They leave unstructured substances or organisms in their wake, as the misshapen organisms, our atomic generators, or our genetic engineering produces in the shape of undeveloped organisms termed mutations.

Both one-sidednesses are the result of a too narrow, merely profit-orientated approach to life. A harmonious state can only come about when an organic state of symbiosis, (the living interpetration of the two opposing principles) occurs and they mutually exercise their forces to hold one another in balance.

But, after this digression, necessary for the understanding of those modern phenomena which occur through the misplacement of emphasis on a too narrow, one-sided aspect of the forces which maintain the balance in life, let us once more return to our theme: Africa.

If Africa needs consciousness-forces, it must take *pain and suffering* into the bargain, that is the price to pay. If one ponders this statement, the question will arise in one's heart, "How can I share, help to carry this heavy burden of Africa's pain? How can I emerge out of my cocoon and learn to say "Yes, how can I change your suffering, how can my actions alleviate it?" Perhaps the question is not even articulated, but nonetheless, it is very real. "What is my brother's need for *his eternal being's* sake? Am I, with all my heart's concern truly open to the subtle language of the Holy Spirit? Is it trying to reach me through his words, through his actions?" And in words of thunder the world answers, "If you do not manage to develop this Spirit-Self attitude of real listening with all the fibres of your heart, all your efforts to work towards the spiritual future of Africa will be in vain. But if you do, then pain will become the systole, and joy the diastole of the circulation of the life-forces of love between man and man, and Africa's liberation from its age-long bondage of having to bear the Atlantean karma of the world, will have at last begun!"

This would seem to be the place to cite a prayer of Christan Morgenstern, a friend of Steiner's, a poet who suffered much pain with great fortitude, until his early death, while still a young man.

> I call thee, pain, with all thy awful might
> Strike this, my heart, that suffering prove its worth
> And, that I am, this humble bit of earth
> Sustains me from the universal night.
>
> I call thee, dearest friend of humankind;
> Mistrust not that I ever thee denied,
> Thou pain, thou didst for us the greatest find,
> That could from man and beast man's own divide.
>
> I call thee: let me drain thy bitter cup;
> Though yet thou seest me turn with falt'ring feet
> As fortune, only, cannot help me up
> Help thou me then my day's work to complete.
>
> — *Christian Morgenstern*

South Africa, the Foot of the Etheric Cross of the World

We spoke of the valley cross inscribed into Africa. A greater valley cross is inscribed into the face of the whole earth. Its vertical beam is the same Great Rift Valley, the greatest north-south trench scoring the surface of the earth. We stated that its foot stopped at Table Mountain. In the North it dips for a time underground, only to reappear as the Dnieper Valley, from which it gradually peters out towards the North. Its lowest point is the Dead Sea, which lies about 396m below the level of the Mediterranean Sea. This is crossed by the greatest east-west trench, the Mediterranean Basin. Its outrunners extend (crossed by the Great Atlantic Ridge) right to the American Great Lakes in the West and, also with interruptions, via the Black and the Caspian Seas up to the Aral Sea and right up to Lake Baikal

132

in the East. At its crossing point lies the Holy Land where Christ walked on earth. (At the Dead Sea, whose surface lies below sea-level we have the place where the surface of the earth comes nearest to its centre). Let us recall the Reciprocal Relationship discussed earlier on. In this sense, this Valley Cross can be understood to be the locus of an etheric cross.

The Etheric Cross of the World

Let us now look at a few images. Do not ask me to "prove" them. Just let them stand and see what your heart says to them. Perhaps you will discover that they will hold up to a higher test than which the intellect can provide, and sustain their inner validity.

At the foot of the World Cross stands Table Mountain like a mighty altar, usually covered by an "Altar Cloth" (the cloud layer which Capetonians call "the Table Cloth"). To the West, looking threateningly towards the East, lies a mountain called the "Lion's Head." To the East, menacing the West lies another called the "Devil's Peak." Do these perhaps suggest the names Lucifer and Ahriman *(see below)*? After all, the Cape is the Cape of Storms. (In ancient times, mariners of the East called it "Cap Diabolo," the Devil's Cape. Are these two "devils" raging against the "Table of the Lord?" And the wall of cliffs falling into the sea beyond the "Lion's Head" is called "The Twelve Apostles." Are they watching what sort of sacrifices are laid before the foot of the "Cross of the World?" The row of the "Twelve Apostles" is brought to a close by a mountain called "Karbonkel-skop," (the Garnet's Head).

Garnet has the colour of pure blood. Yet, the geological formation, a part of the "Table Mountain Series," consists of sandstone, which does not produce garnets. Nonetheless, will this one day, not by nature's means but by man's achievement, sparkle as a beacon, translucent as the incarnate Blood of Christ? Will the Cape's new name, "The Cape of the Good Hope" of the world then be truly earned?

Nomen est Omen! Do not touch this image with the sacrilegious hands of the intellect, simply let it stand.

Let us define two more concepts necessary for our understanding.

The Two Great Adversaries of
Lucifer and Ahriman

On his path of development, man has to steer a middle course between the Scylla and Charybdis of these two mighty, opposing spiritual beings.

The one, in anthroposophical terminology, is called **Lucifer:** the light wants to lead man towards beauty, to the spirit, towards self-development, but in an egoistical way, separating him from his fellow men. In lulling man's social conscience to sleep, Lucifer tries to lure man away from his earthly responsibilities, to alienate him from community with his fellow men. One could say that Lucifer tries to keep man in a spiritual womb-like state and prevents him from entering the earth by working in it. Nonetheless, *man cannot develop spiritually without Lucifer's powers.* It is when Man one-sidedly abandons himself to Lucifer's influence that he becomes *proud and morally endangered.*

Lucifer is opposed by another mighty spiritual power whom Anthroposophy calls **Ahriman:** (the Bible refers to him as "The great beast" or as "Satan" or "Beelzebub"). Man needs Ahriman's powers to think logically; to understand and manipulate the physical substances of the earth. All modern technology (for instance the word-processor on which this article is being written!) is literally unthinkable without his powers. We need him for the awakening of our earthly awareness. However, like Lucifer, he does not act altruistically. He would like to harden, to enslave man's spirit in materialism. He is not anti-social, quite the contrary, he tries to enmesh men, ant-like, as cogs in social machines — in bureaucracies, mass production, on conveyor belts, etc. He tries to anaesthetise man by means of the mass media, to drown his spirit-consciousness in floods of irrelevant information until man loses his orientation and *forgets that he is a spiritual being.* We need Ahriman's help to understand and master the forces of the earth; but woe to man's spirit if he abandons the reins and lets Ahriman take over. He becomes a prey to fear.

134

Only **Christ** can give man the strength to steer a middle course. Nailed to the cross, thereby irreversibly committed to and dying into the earth; rising again in the resurrection and going to the heavenly Father — to the realm of the spirit; His loving hands outstretched to man right to the very end — there is no grander vision of the helper along the middle path. Down the ages Africa hs been held in thrall between Lucifer and Ahriman. Ahriman so hardened the earth, that man fled into Lucifer's arms and did not fully come down to earth with his consciousness. With few exceptions (such as Egypt and Abyssinia, the "Ethiopia" of "Prester John"), whose cultures are not truly African in origin, men have not cultivated the earth and have produced hardly any great cultural monuments. They have not changed, transformed the earth and made it 'their own', individualised home. It was Ahriman who, so hardened nature (and men's bodies and life-forces,) that he could hold man in his vice-grip of fear. Man's consciousness could not break through to become fully awake spirit-awareness. In Africa man's consciousness wanders in a dream land between heaven and earth, bereft of the sure knowledge of his spiritual origin, nor secure against the many threatening dangers on earth.

Fear haunts everyone, the homeless; fear and superstition also haunt the wanderer. Read the poem of creation in Credo Mutwa's *Indaba My Children* (only printed in the first edition; unfortunately it has been omitted in later editions). Anyone acquainted with the spiritual history of the world, as given by Steiner in his *Outline of Occult Science* will be amazed how accurately Mutwa's pictures reflect the spiritual history of the earth. In reading Mutwa's book one is left with one overriding impression: fear pervades it from beginning to end. Fear is almost tangible: it is omnipresent in the attitude of the moon-goddess, the tree of life inspires it, fear of demonically threatening nature spirits, fear of headmen, fear of chiefs, fear of other tribes. Fear has divided Africa's people, fear has co-agulated nations into fear ruled empires; fear is everywhere!

Fear rules the whole of modern Africa. To a diminishing degree it still rules in South Africa which is but slowly emerging from under its cloud. Indeed, fear reaches out and influences *all* world relations,

135

fear it is one of the pillars of world-wide apartheid. As long as we allow fear to stop the human exchange of heart forces, the flow of soul-forces between man and man, the divisive Ahrimanic forces will rule us and the world. *Trust* — not blind trust, but trust imbued with the Consciousness-Self attitude of seeking to recognise the working of Christ in my neighbour's spirit, this is the trust that can overcome Ahriman's rule. [13]

St George and the Dragon

As we have spoken about the dragon of human fear, it may be appropriate to close with the counter-image of St George — the image of man inspired by St Michael, fighting the dragon.

The legend tells us that St George was sleeping somewhere in Arabia, when St Michael appeared to him and commanded him to go to rescue a princess in distress. Her father's land had been ravaged by a mighty sea dragon which had swallowed all cattle and sheep and whose fiery breath would scorch all the land unless he was given a virgin to devour. Many virgins had already fallen prey to him when, at last, the lot fell on the king's daughter, the princess. The king pleaded to exempt her, his only child, but the populace demurred. In the end the princess herself overrode his objections and out of her own free will went to sacrifice herself to the dragon.

As soon as the vision had passed, St George roused himself, mounted his steed, and rode off to rescue the princess. He found her, tied up by the side of the sea, dismally awaiting her fate. Ignoring her entreaties to flee, he told her to wake him up when the dragon appeared. Thereupon he laid himself down to sleep, resting his head in her lap. At last the dragon came over the waves. As soon as he was woken up by the princess, St George sprang onto his horse and fought a long and fierce battle. He only conquered the dragon when he managed to pierce his throat with his lance. Thereupon he fastened the princess' girdle to its shaft (note, he did not kill the dragon!). Thereupon the dragon, now quite tame, followed her "like an obedient lapdog."

St George then took her back up the mountain to her father and, declining any reward, he rode on his way.

What does this legend tell us? What does the imagery of mythology have to say about this? He asks the princess to wake him up, that is, he is to use his clear, awake consciousness. He employs a horse (a horse in the language of mythology always represents the power of man's thinking) for his battle. The lance pierces a hole into the dragon's dark hide and lets in light, the daylight of consciousness. Thus he overcomes the dragon of fear. The sea (water) is an image for the etheric, i.e. the life-forces; the dragon's fiery breath that scorches and destroys is a picture of his uncontrolled passions, i.e. his wild, and therefore destructive astral forces. The dragon, sailing across the water, is thus an image of the unholy combination of astral and etheric forces in the form of drives, which have devastated the continent of old Atlantis. It is thus a representative of the unresolved Atlantean conflicts, of Atlantean karma overcome by a man (St. George) carrying Michaelic consciousness into the dragon. The princess always represents man's higher, his future self. Now St. George can tie man's unpolluted, virginal astral forces (the princess' girdle) to the dragon and thereby tame him. His throat, fulminating his dark, instinct-nature is pierced by Michaelic light, and, tamed, can now serve man's higher being i.e. follow the princess "like an obedient lap-dog"; he now serves man's will. "Up the hill" means: man returns to the father, to his spiritual home. It is a true picture of the redemption of man. St. George, the Michaelic hero, does not need a reward, the redemption of man's higher being is that, he needs no other. The dragon also had suffered. By St George's lance brings him consciousness and he can again serve man's development, with newfound awareness serve man's pure soul forces.

The age old suffering of the heart of Africa must be taken on with the heart's power of sacrifice and pierced, illumined with St Michael's lance of Christian esoteric wisdom — out of this the future will be born.

137

REFERENCES

1   Rudolf Steiner: *The Foundation Stone* - Anthroposophical Publ. Co. London.

2   See Theodor Schwenk: *Sensitive Chaos* - Freies Geistesleben, Stuttgart.

3   See Schwenk's photographs of water-currents in *The Sensitive Chaos* and Excerpts of his work in the Weleda Calendar 1963 - Weleda A.G. Schwäb. Gmünd

4   See Jen & Des Bartlett - *Nature's Paradise*: Pages 106-108. Collins, London

5   See the voluminous literature by Steiner and other anthroposophical writers on these subjects, especially: Ernst Marti - Das Aetherische, Die Pforte Verlag, im Rudolf Steiner Verlag, Dornach, Switzerland

6   See the voluminous literature by Steiner and other anthroposophical writers.

7   Rudolf Steiner: *Reincarnation and Karma* etc. - Rudolf Steiner Press, London.

8   Rudolf Steiner: *An Outline of Occult Science , The Theosophy of the Rosecrucians.*

9   Credo Vusamazulu Mutwa: *Indaba My Children*, 1st edition, Blue Crane Books,Johannesburg.

10   Richard St Barbe Baker: *My Life My Trees* - Findhorn Publications. Also by the same author: *Sahara Challenge and Sahara Conquest.*

11   Rudolf Steiner: *Anthroposophical Leading Thoughts* Rudolf Steiner Press, London.

12   Rudolf Steiner: *Historical Phenomenology* - Rudolf Steiner Press. London.

13   As said above, such statements merely try to highlight a general background. Of course there are, and always have been individual exceptions. For instance: the writer is convinced that many medicine men - of whom Mutwa is a striking example - have profound knowledge, not in abstract terms, but in pictorial form, appropriate to Africa. Also leaders have emerged such as Nelson Mandela, who have risen above fear and inspire faith in the future.

Chapter 9

Ubuntu in Africa

Mfuniselwa John Bhengu

W HILE MOST OF AFRICA is pre-occupied with its separate and individual development efforts, East Africa — particularly Somalia, Rwanda, Burundi and Sudan — has experienced violence of the worst kind. The solution to these upheavals necessitates a multi-faceted approach, but particularly development of the spirit of Ubuntu.

These upheavals are not new in the East African region but they are qualitatively different from those elsewhere in Africa. In other parts of the continent revolutionary upheavals are mostly deliberate, disciplined and organised, with the exception of Liberia. The genocide in both Burundi and Rwanda was unforeseen even by the African Commission on Human and Peoples' Rights, which has monitored human rights abuses in Rwanda since 1990 — well before the 1994 genocide. Early warnings of this kind have also been available in Burundi.

There have been many gross violations of human and peoples' rights in recent years in Africa. In fact, the number of human rights emergencies in Africa is on the increase. The list of nations which have had emergencies — from civil wars and ethnic violence to human rights abuses by the state — includes Algeria, Angola, Burundi, Congo, Ghana, Kenya, Liberia, Mali, Mauritania, Niger, Nigeria, Rwanda, Sierra Leone, Somalia, Sudan and Zaire. This deadly "social engineering" for political purposes needs to be stopped forthwith because it is the antithesis of Ubuntu (African Humanism).

The intention behind Article 58 of the Organisation for African Unity's (OAU's) Commission on Human and Peoples' Rights, which came into force in 1987, is to ensure that there is ample warning about degenerating human rights situations and that there is a mechanism in place to try and prevent these situations from worsening. Although the intention is to protect human rights, this Commission does not have enforcement or executive powers and its role is limited to making recommendations to the OAU assembly. As a mechanism to help prevent human rights violations in Africa, the Commission lacks human and material resources to prevent human rights abuses taking place on the continent.

Clearly a collective African wisdom is more imperative now than ever before. The wisdom of African leaders such as former Tanzanian president Julius Nyerere, the OAU Secretary-General Salim-Ahmed Salim, and many others should be pooled. This is an African problem that needs an African solution directed by African leaders.

The launch in Arusha on 13th March 1996 of the East African Cooperation (EAC), is an event to be hailed not only by East Africans themselves, but by all Africans who should view such a step as contributing towards the broader and long-term goal of an African Economic Community. The EAC may also be able to develop the abilities, currently lacking in the OAU, to combat human rights abuses.

Burundi is in civil war right now. It is an ethnic civil war. It has a new undemocratic government — a Tutsi government that overthrew the previous democratically elected government, and millions of Hutus have fled the country in fear of their lives. Many countries,

140

both in Africa and in Europe have now imposed sanctions on Burundi. But the question that comes to the minds of the people is: Why is it that Africa is not recognising the new Burundi government, yet Africa for decades has had military coups de tat, for example in Nigeria ? African leaders never said a word when General Abacha of Nigeria overthrew the previous democratically elected government of Nigeria. They (African leaders) never held an Arusha conference to determine what steps they were going to take against Nigeria, as they have now done in the Burundi situation.

Africa needs peace initiatives more than ever before, and it is hoped that the idea of an African Human Rights Court which has been mooted by African leaders recently will strengthen the efforts of the Commission on Human and Peoples' Rights to bring political stability to Africa. But the African Human Rights Court will have to embrace the spirit of Ubuntu (African Humanism) if it is going to succeed and be effective. Soul and spiritual problems need soul and spiritual medicine, not just another social technique. It is gratifying that Julius Nyerere is a facilitator in this process, because the African Human Rights Court could benefit much from him as one the few African leaders who knows the effectiveness of the spirit of Ubuntu.

But what is Ubuntu? Ubuntu is the humanistic experience of treating all people with respect, granting them their human dignity. It encompasses values like universal brotherhood, sharing and respect for other people as human beings. It is a belief in sacredness, and is the foremost priority of the human being in all conduct; it is a lifelong process.

The Ubuntu philosophy displays tolerance. It displays awareness of what is just and unjust; what is humane and inhumane; an awareness of the distinction between kindness and cruelty; between harmony and disharmony; appreciation of peace over war; love over violence and hatred; appreciation of life over death. Ubuntu, therefore, is completely contrary to inhuman behaviour. Ubuntu is the art of being human - a desirable state which contributes positively towards sustaining the well-being of a people, community or society. Ubuntu is active and adaptable. It is a respect for human dignity; sharing of

141

the resources; work by everyone and exploitation by none. It is a cradle for peace and development. It is the essence of democracy.

Humanism in thought demands humanism in deed. The whole of the African traditional life-style with its age-sets, rites of passage and several generations living together, is built on the principle that "you cannot be human alone." Our humanity finds fulfilment only in community with others. Basic to this African idea of community is the African 'experience' of Ubuntu (personhood). To say a human being is a radiating, relations-seeking force is, in fact, verbalising an analysis of an experience. Human beings, single or in groups, are not dead plastic matter which can be scaled and measured at will, neither sheep nor goats driven and tossed hither and thither.

Africa, especially East African countries that have had and are having political upheavals resulting in genocide and human rights abuses, should know that whomsoever kills another human being, has also killed all of human kind, and whomsoever saves a human life, has saved all of human kind. The important point to remember is that every person can improve himself and should be given the opportunity to do so, however serious his mistakes may have been. The reason for this is that deep down inside each human being there exists the potential for development towards the highest good. To commit murder would totally destroy that potentiality. Capital punishment is not a correction; it can only be an act of revenge. In executing someone, we rule out irrevocably any possibility of moral development and of the growth of conscience. I have no doubt that the humane treatment of even a murderer will enhance man's dignity and make society more human. This is what Ubuntu demands.

When the world's nations came together about five decades ago to found the United Nations (UN), few reminders were needed of what could happen when a state believed that there was no limit to what it could do to human beings. The staggering extent of state brutality and terror during World War II and the consequences for people throughout the world were still unfolding in December 1948, when the UN General Assembly adopted without dissent the Universal Declaration of Human Rights.

This Declaration is a pledge among nations to promote fundamental rights as the foundation of freedom, justice and peace. The rights it proclaims are inherent in every human being. They are not privileges that may be granted by governments for good behaviour and they may not be withdrawn for bad behaviour. Fundamental human rights limit what a state may do to a man, woman or child. This is totally in line with the teachings of Ubuntu philosophy.

Killing denies the value of human life. By violating the right to life, it removes the foundation for the realisation of all rights enshrined in the Universal Declaration of Human Rights. The right to life is the supreme right from which no derogation is permitted even in time of public emergency which threatens the life of the nation. In Amnesty International's view, for example, "No one shall be subjected to torture or to cruel, inhuman or degrading treatment or punishment". Ubuntu is similarly against any violations of human rights.

Professor Ali Mazrui summed up Africa's plight when delivering a speech in Johannesburg recently, saying: "Africa was experiencing a high-risk rebellion not only against the post-colonial state but sometimes against the state per se as a mode of government. Many African societies were ill at ease with the state as a system of governance. But behind all the scenarios and the search for solutions, behind the pain and the anguish, is the paramount question - are we facing birth pangs or death pangs in the present African crisis? Is this blood from the womb of history, giving painful birth to a new order?"

It has become increasingly evident that the establishment of an African peace-keeping structure to pre-empt and manage conflict is long overdue. But for that peace-keeping structure to be effective and have impact, it needs to embrace the philosophy of Ubuntu. It has to be spiritually motivated not by any particular religion but by the spirit of Ubuntu. The African continent is affected by many problems. Some of the problems arise from the legacies of colonialism, while some are inherent in the systems and institutions which Africa created in the post-colonial era. To solve these immense problems Africa needs a collective wisdom which uses multi-faceted peace initiatives coupled with the infusion of Ubuntu philosophy.

The words of Dr David Nicol, the Sierra Leonese scholar, should ring a bell for the East African countries: " We have looked across a vast continent and dared to call it ours. You are not a country, Africa, you are a concept which we all fashion in our minds." Dr Nicol was emphasising the fact that Africa derives her nature not only from geography, but also from her people. We talk of Africa and her identity. We refer to her children. This identity is unique because it regards Africa as a concept or value, precisely in the way that it recognises each one of her children as a self-defining value. The focus is on the African culture, its evaluation of the person and its attitude to the human being.

What is needed now is a new consciousness or revelation in which the Spirit of Ubuntu becomes the leading image of all development. A social development in which fear is replaced by joy, insecurity by confidence, materialism by spiritual values and anti-social behaviour by Ubuntu. This transformation is necessary for Africa and the whole world if we wish to stem the current social and economic slide into chaos.

The need of our deeply troubled world is for the Holy Spirit, called in the New Testament, the Comforter to come and bring Ubuntu to the hearts and minds of the people. May we be filled with this Spirit of Ubuntu and rise into a new consciousness of our brothers and sisters to become worthy of Ubuntu

Chapter 10

The Servant Leader, a Peaceful Alternative for a Continent at War

Ralph Shepherd

The Servant Leader

Since the middle of the 1960's the western world has witnessed the gradual disappearance of the 'strong leader' — the archetypal boss who carried the authority, held the vision, gave the commands, supervised the action and dealt out the rewards or retribution[1]. This disappearance of the leader in both the political and corporate life seemed to announce a change in general management and leadership and has been the subject of numerous articles in Time Magazine[2] and elsewhere.

This phenomenon of the lack of strong leadership is not however evidenced in the same way in the Third World, and particularly in Africa where innumerable strong personalities ranging from gangster bosses and local warlords to heads-of-state abound. As to whether they are good leaders is altogether another consideration.

The First World problem of the lack of leadership has led to a certain amount of apathy in the political sphere, and is regarded as part of the cause in the decline of the economic life whilst the egotistic self-interest of strong personalities in Africa who are able to solicit (or coerce!) followers, is seen as part cause of the ongoing fighting throughout the strife torn continent.

At a superficial level, the leadership problems of the First World and Third World plus their attendant woes seem diametrically opposed and therefore require different remedies. The common approach to the problem of leadership in First World countries is the proliferation of leadership development programmes conducted by universities and business houses, whilst in the Third World — and particularly in Africa — the gun is seen as the solution! Neither of the so-called solutions have had any effect except to create more distress. The First World is still bereft of leaders whilst for every gangster boss or dictator assassinated in the Third World, there are many more to claim, and fight over, the vacancy created.

Laurens van der Post in conversation with Jean-Marc Pottiez[3] shared the following, "We often ask ourselves why there is no religious leader appearing to deliver us from stagnation and retrogression with some shattering new revelation? Why is there no great statement of cosmic intent which we can all try to follow? What has happened to all these great minds and leaders who used to guide leaders in the past? The answer is clear: the stage of great leaders is irrevocably gone and the task, the responsibility, is tossed onto each one of us. We are in our own theatre alone. We have to wake our own sense of what is collective individual, and live as individuals following the truth as our own nature's predispose us."

If the advice of Laurens van der Post is not taken seriously, is the West to lapse into a directionless socio-economic apathetic muddle, whilst the African continent slides into perpetual war or, if we do wake to the situation and Sir Laurens' advice is heeded, is there a procedure or course of action that will address both types of leadership problems referred to above? A healthy alternative that addresses the fundamental cause of the problems and not just the symptoms?

During the 1960's many management consultants and advisors together with university research groups worked on these questions. Among those dedicated people one man, working over decades, developed the concept of the Servant-Leader as a possible new paradigm in leadership and management that would address the problems of both the First World and Third or majority world's lack of leadership.

In 1991 Robert Greenleaf, the originator of the Servant-Leader concept, died, leaving behind him a legacy that could in time change not only corporate America, but business practice and organisational management world-wide. Robert's legacy is now working as the Robert Greenleaf Foundation for the development and promotion of the Servant-Leadership Paradigm. This new paradigm in management and leadership is applicable to all institutions and community organisations when new forms and directions are being sought to replace the out-moded and no longer effective management and leadership models described by Alvin Toffler[4] as belonging to Second Wave management styles. Robert Greenleaf worked for more than thirty years for the American Telephone & Telecommunications Company (known to the world as AT&T) in its management organisation and training division. AT&T employ over two million people and is the largest corporate employer in America, and possibly the world.

Greenleaf retired as AT&T's director of Management Research, where, out of his long years of experience in management training, he developed the concept of the Servant-Leader as the foundation for what has now become, a new paradigm in corporate and organisational management.

In order to lead effectively in the future, Greenleaf suggests that a 'leader' must first and foremost be a 'servant', or have the qualities of a servant, that is, to be able to recognise the highest priority needs[5] of others and to be humble to the task and not proud of the position (of being a leader).

In our Western society with its materialistic and egotistic values, based largely upon acquisitiveness, control and competition, such a concept as the Servant-Leader requires not only a change of attitude of management function, but a fundamental change in the way in which we think.

New Paradigms

The questions we can ask ourselves are : can we think and conceptualise in a new way? And, is there evidence of such change in consciousness in the past to support this possibility? A consideration of socio-cultural change from the late Middle Ages in Europe into the Renaissance is one example. The transition from a spirit-centred world view to the mechanistic Cartesian world view during the seventeenth century is a better one. The next questions we can ask ourselves are: does a new paradigm shift in consciousness in humankind come in its own time or can its coming be fostered? Is the world-wide proliferation of books and seminars on change a sign of the birth of a new consciousness or are they a symptomatic outcome of the problems themselves? Or both?

The Robert Greenleaf Foundation is one such non profit organisation, that offers specialised training programmes, consultancy, books and videos, to further the development of Servant-Leadership as a management concept within the corporate world. The growth of this paradigm in management training is shared now by other leaders in this field. Dr Stephen Covey in his books *The Seven Habits of Highly Effective People* and *Principle Centred Leadership*[6] also contributes to the concept of Servant-Leadership, as do fellow American organisational development consultants Peter Senge and Tom Peters.

Before we examine further the paradigm of the Servant-Leader, we should give some consideration to the historical background and current cultural conditions in the world, in particular the business and corporate communities. Consideration should also be given to the nature of human consciousness within the cultures we live in. The development and growth of both consciousness and culture are fundamental to the acceptance and rejection of new ideas or paradigms. Many discoveries in science had to wait for long periods of time until the general consciousness and culture had evolved sufficiently to receive them.

Five or six hundred years before the Christian era, Hero of Alexandra developed a primitive steam engine but the times — consciousness and culture — were not ready to receive it. Two thousand years had still to pass before Thomas Savery came along and built the first steam engine that was to have a practical use. Ten years ago (1985) in the 'Old' South Africa, the concept of Majority Rule was considered untenable and impossible by many white South Africans. Today, those same people who once supported the principle of apartheid can't understand how apartheid could have come into being in the first place! There are many other examples where ideas failed only because they were ahead of their time. The inventions of Leonardo da Vinci like the helicopter, is another example.

The concept of the Servant-Leader seen against the background of today's leadership crisis, seems now relevant and appropriate for our time as we observe new social and other paradigms appearing on the world stage. When a new idea manifests and is received, it can be said to have come at the 'right time' and possibly be part of, if not a new paradigm shift in itself. The works of Robert Greenleaf, Stephen Covey, Peter Senge, Rudolf Steiner and many other modern thinkers are now finding expression in Victor Hugo's statement "There is nothing as powerful as an idea whose time has come!"

But what is a 'new paradigm'? It seems that we can't imagine it, we can't foresee it; the collapse of Communism — which we will discuss later — and of the Berlin Wall are good examples. They took us all by surprise! A new paradigm has been described as "A new vision of reality, a fundamental change in our thoughts, perceptions and values."[7]

149

It seems that all the enormous changes in the political, social and economic spheres of humankind indicate that a new paradigm in the development of human relationships is beginning to show itself in the Western world, a paradigm in which truly spirit-centred values are replacing materialistic ones. Values in which relationships are at last becoming more important than 'things'; whether those things are titles, positions or possessions. Peter Senge of MIT describes, in a video presentation on Servant-Leadership, how our Western desire for 'things' manifested in the scientific search for the atom. The atom being the ultimate 'thing' upon which the substance of matter was considered to be built. However, now at the end of the century, science tells us that the concept of the atom as the ultimate piece of matter does not correspond to what is now experienced by scientists. There is no matter where the atom is, only empty space in which ever changing energy relationships interweave.

This realisation that what seemed to be substance made up of tiny pieces of matter — atoms — is in reality only empty space has come as a shock to the western mind. For the past four centuries matter has replaced the spiritual world view as the only reality; now we are told that our senses have been deluding us, for matter, in reality, does not exist! Or not at least in the form in which we previously conceived it.

Peter Senge — as did Rudolf Steiner seventy years before him — elaborates on the impermanence of the physical body in his video presentation mentioned above, by drawing our attention to the fact that the average life span of a human cell is only two years! Even our own bodies that seem to us to be so real, are in a constant state of flux between dissolving and becoming. What then keeps us looking the way we do? To take this thought one step further we can also consider that approximately 85% of our body mass is water, and that this water content changes completely every two weeks yet we still look the same. Where then is the 'architect' that holds the form of our body together? In fact we can ask the same question about organic form whether that be in the human, animal or plant kingdoms. Somewhere else other than the physical realm!

The saying "There is nothing as permanent as change" allows us the courage to consider new paradigms in all spheres of human endeavour in which set ways of thinking — Cartesian mechanistic — can be transcended in order to develop new capacities and even new bodily or soul senses for the coming culture.

Management

Stephen Covey — the world renowned organisation and development consultant — describes four basic management paradigms[8] that have developed during this century. The first Covey calls 'the scientific management paradigm' in which a total authoritarian type leader, the Boss, gives the commands and makes all the decisions to which employees have to conform and co-operate as requested in order to receive their pay and other benefits. This form of leadership is still probably the dominant style of leadership or management, particularly in the Third World in both the political and business spheres of society.

The second management paradigm described by Stephen Covey as appearing for the first time in the 1930's is the 'human relations paradigm' in which managers now recognise that workers or employees are also social beings with feelings and emotions, and treat them with kindness, civility, decency and courtesy. The management style is still authoritarian; the boss is still the boss.

During the 1960's a third paradigm in management appeared, one in which people were now seen also as psychological beings, in which their involvement in development was recognised as a resource. We now begin to observe a move away from authoritarianism towards a more inclusive and participatory management style. This has been called the human resources paradigm in which the talents and abilities are recognised and used. The result of this showed a marked development in efficiency and excellence. Yet the manager still leads, with kindness and inclusivity, but the style is still top-down!

Stephen Covey then describes the birth of the fourth paradigm which he calls Principle Centred Leadership. This paradigm is not just an advancement on the previous three, it is a radically altered state of awareness in which the view of the employer being above or higher than the workers, as experienced in the previous paradigms, has changed to that of being a co-worker or facilitator with them – in fact, the word *employee* also changes in favour of the word *associate*. This new development or paradigm in management, can also be described as the Servant-Leader in which the leader or manager recognises not only the physical or psychological needs of the employee/associates, but sees them also as spiritual beings that have meaning in their own right as human beings. Associate/employees also contribute their ideas to the future building of the organisation. Such a recognition and participation does not diminish the responsibility of the manager/leader to lead, but he no longer instructs, he inspires. Experience has shown that this new paradigm imparts to employees/associates the sense of ownership for no longer as in previous paradigms is there participation in the organisation based solely on what they can contribute, but upon their own inner sense of purpose, thereby imparting dignity instead of servility.

Principle Centred Leadership dramatically enhances the performance of the organisation in quality, efficiency, effectiveness and excellence. Workers no longer feel that they are merely working for a living, but that working itself becomes meaningful. Through their work, purpose and personal challenge provides the environment in which they can grow as human beings. Scott Bader of the Scott Bader Commonwealth[9] was one of the pioneers of this management paradigm in the 1950's and 60's. However, it has also been practised in Quaker based organisations, like Cadbury's U.K. Ltd.

Another pioneer in new management forms is Semco, Brazil's largest marine and food processing machinery manufacturer[10]. Semco is run on purely democratic principles. Employee/associates are actively involved in all decision making and determine their own salaries based upon market awareness and profitability. The success and growth of Semco is based upon the ethic of giving employees/associates control over their own lives.

Another success story of humanised enterprises is Anita Roddick's The Body Shop[11] with over 700 branches in 37 countries. The natural raw materials purchased for The Body Shops are purposely bought from Third World countries with the company slogan "Trade Not Aid." Through this process, The Body Shop people are assisting the development in these countries. "What we are trying to do" says Anita Roddick, "is to create a new business paradigm simply showing that businesses can have a more human face and social conscience."

Both Ricardo Semler of Semco and Anita Roddick have developed their enterprises as Servant-Leaders and have demonstrated with others like Robert Greenleaf and Scott Bader, that the time for the new paradigm of Servant-Leadership has come.

Community Upliftment

A Servant-Leader managed organisation exhibits an entirely different relationship to the community at large compared to traditional commercial concerns whose only motive for existing is to make profits. Organisations operating out of the new paradigm in business management exhibit greater awareness of their responsibility to community needs and have well developed social responsibility programmes in which staff members play an active part and are profitable enterprises as well. In South Africa, the Otis Elevator Company is one example where the employees are encouraged to participate in management decisions and are actively involved in community projects. It is the employees who determine the support for social projects and become actively involved in their execution.

Such organisations can radically transform positively the community or environment in which they function. This stands in contrast to organisations that are only concerned with making profits for their shareholders, who still treat their staff as functional employees to serve the needs of the company. Such organisations show little or minimal interest in community support and development.

The Principle-Centred Leadership paradigm transforms the social isolation brought about by the Cartesian world outlook, which promoted a scarcity mentality, into a co-operative and socially concerned activity which naturally promotes an abundance mentality.

This new paradigm in management reveals not just a change in emphasis — i.e. gradually decreasing authoritarianism — but a bold shift in our basic values. Our Western materialistic culture largely places value and ownership on 'things' that can be acquired, whereas the shift in consciousness brought about by this new paradigm fosters new values, or rather reawakens dormant ones, values that have a truly spiritual basis. From such foundations the emphasis is placed upon harmonising and developing relationships. This shift in consciousness does not in any way diminish the value, advances and benefits of our technological age. It only seeks to bring a balance to our consumer consciousness though a developed attitude of stewardship of the Earth. Such a healthy attitude balances the industrial consumption of raw materials with ecological regeneration by, for example, planting more trees than we cut down. We can see the beginning of this attitude of caring in companies like The Body Shop, or Cape Town's Golden Arrow Bus Company which are directed to long term gains on a win-win basis as opposed to short term profit taking on a win-lose basis.

Social Responsibility

Over the past twenty years, many South African companies voluntarily instituted social responsibility programmes, whilst the few American companies that remained active during the last decades of the apartheid era, were forced by American law to adhere to the Sullivan Code, which prescribed active social responsibility programmes. Now that South Africa has a new democratic government installed, many companies have stopped their social responsibility programmes, thereby indicating that the time for business in partnership with the community is over. The dissolving of the Urban Foundation as a project-based development organisation brought about by some of the captains of South African industry seems to confirm this. For some established organisations the old paradigms still hold sway; unfortunately it seems that we will witness the effects of this entrenched second-wave business style in continued strikes and other industrial disturbances as workers compete with employers for the benefits of their labour.

Shortly after South Africa's first democratic elections in April

1994, many large organisations were plagued with strikes, with the effects of damaging the productivity of the organisations in question. All that was achieved by the workers was a meagre percentage rise in salary, no more than what they would have got without the strike. Some companies were forced into liquidation. All around it was a lose-lose situation. Progressive companies like Tetra Pak in Natal, which have introduced Principle-Centred leadership and educational programmes, were free of industrial disputes. Tetra Pak have been able to involve their workforce in such a way that they really feel that they, as individuals, do matter.

Some Cape wine farmers have begun issuing shares to their workers who now enjoy sharing in the profits of the harvest. The Golden Arrow Bus company have gone one step further than just issuing shares to the employees, they have donated 50% of the company's assets to their own social responsibility trust!

Courage to Let Go

The great changes reflected in the evolution of consciousness in history, seems to be spasmodic, in other words they often happen unexpectedly. Conversely, some shifts are anticipated. The changes expected at the end of this century have been debated and speculated about since the 1920's and before. Changes of this kind are often painful for the unprepared, for when a new paradigm replaces an old one, something has to be given up. Old, seemingly secure and cherished opinions and wishes held for many years, or decades of academic research, appear to be suddenly swept away when, what was believed to be the "Truth" is suddenly radically altered through new discoveries. When horse-drawn power gave way to steam, steam to the electrical industrial age, rote learning to information resources centre learning, great strides had also to be taken in the development of human consciousness to cope with or adjust to the new culture that came with the changes.

In the global business community this phenomenon of rapid change is now well known. Suddenly a prized and well-developed product becomes obsolete overnight[12]. Many American companies have ex-

155

perienced this in recent years and have been able to shift their corporate dedication from that based solely on profits or product identification, to that of their own human resources, their employees.

Harrison Owen, an international leading organisation and development consultant, has successfully developed training programmes to assist corporations face and prepare for change[13]. When a company's product was no longer marketable, but there still existed a well-trained and dedicated staff including production engineers, marketing and public relations, administration and finance personnel, the question is "Why don't we keep the team and change the product?" In the past factories closed because their products became obsolete; now it is a matter of re-educating the staff to see what is required in the market place. Brazil's Semco, mentioned above, has a team of researchers whose sole function is to continually explore the new, whether the 'new' be in the form of innovative change to production, or new products themselves. Because of this team, Semco has been able to maintain its position in the forefront of company development in Brazil.

In order for companies to move into the future, it is important for the workforce to be dedicated to working together as a team. Re-education of employees and commitment to a shared, and well developed, mission statement are fundamental to organisations working in a continually changing world. Stephen Covey's Principle Centred Leadership enables the entire staff to experience ownership of the enterprise, as do the workers in Semco, to the point that they are prepared to take collective risks that would send uncommitted people rushing to look for another job (if another exists!).

To move from one paradigm to another requires not only a change in consciousness, but re-education as well. When Scott Bader took his company on the journey from a family owned top-down managed business in 1945 to a full staff owned 'commonwealth' in 1962, he preceded this development with rigorous education and training programmes. For an employee to be a shareholder and bear the responsibility of a shareholder, that shareholder must know how to read a balance sheet and understand management principles, even if that staff member is a junior clerical assistant. Each member of the Scott Bader Commonwealth (SBC) had to learn what made a company run efficiently. This principle of ongoing education or what is now termed, "life-long education," seems fundamental to the new culture that is beginning to emerge.

During the 1994 April elections in South Africa, millions of rands were made available from both South African and foreign donors to pay for "voter education." The preparation of South Africa's voters to exercise their right to vote, is only the beginning. Now much more is required to prepare the citizens of South Africa for a new culture with new values if the country is not to deteriorate to the state experienced in other parts of Africa. It seems that unless a political revolution is followed by a cultural revolution — not in the Chinese sense — the indications described in George Orwell's *Animal Farm* will apply and the 'pigs' will take over and the oppression of the people will be worse than before.

At this stage in South Africa's development we have to — and the social and economic conditions allow us — choose upon what principles and values our future culture may be based. Do we want a First World culture based upon consumerism, thereby allowing economic disparity between the haves and the have-nots to continue? Do we want to continue to exploit the mineral resources in the way in which the developed countries have? Or should we go back to an agrarian subsistence economy like so many Third World countries in which hunger, disease and poverty determine population growth? Or do we have the courage to commit ourselves to take a cultural stride, a cultural paradigm shift that can bring to birth an alternative which is neither a First World, nor a Third World nor even a compromise of the two, but which is a new culture in which the principles of real democracy and freedom, together with the resulting responsibility holds sway in human relations; or in which stewardship of the land matches consumption of materials and where fraternity and co-operation are the hallmarks of economic endeavour? Can we consider the results of our actions on future generations? The American Hopi Indians consider the consequences of their deeds on how it would

157

affect in time right through to the seventh generation! The conditions seem right, indications show that a change in consciousness is now dawning. Do we have, or how do we acquire the courage to take this step? One of the most impressive indicators of change was the address given to The World Economic Forum in Davos, Switzerland in February 1992 by the then President of the Czechoslovak Republic, Vaclav Havel, on the collapse of communism and its meaning in our time. The end of communism and the events that followed it is a prime example of one of those major shifts that has taken the world by surprise.

The Beginning

Even a superficial consideration of history reveals the archetype of the servant-leader to be no less than the Being of the Christ. His life on earth during the three years of His ministry from the age thirty to thirty three introduces into human history an entirely new human relations paradigm. In every respect Christ was the servant of the people, yet at the same time He was their leader too. His work transcended religious, national, and cultural boundaries, but it was the picture of the Last Supper that stands as the archetypal picture of The Servant-Leader in which the Christ first washed the feet of His disciples, then sat at the table with them, not at the head as the boss, but with them as a colleague and a brother.

The qualities of Christ's servant-leadership have however been demonstrated in many great spiritual leaders since His time on earth. The Great Prayer of St. Francis of Assisi could well be seen as a manifesto for servant-leaders ..."grant that I may understand and not need to be understood..." During the thousand years following Christ's life, a yearning began to grow in the hearts of people oppressed by wars, enslaved by cruel rulers and restricted by the iron dogmas of the Church, to find a realisation of Christ's Kingdom on earth. So it was upon fertile ground that the legends of the existence of a Christian realm ruled by a Priest-King called John was received. Carried by the returning pilgrims from the Holy Land, the legend of Prester John spread through Europe as the Priest-King in Africa ruling a kingdom as a servant to his people, in which the Christian ethics of brotherhood and caring stood in stark contrast to the harsh rigidity of politics and religion in Europe at the time. The stories of the servant-leadership of Prester John inspired many thousands to begin the search for this Christian African realm. In particular, it was the Portuguese Templars under their new name, The Order of Christ who adopted this search for Prester John as their mission under the leadership of Henry the Navigator. The consequence of the mission of the Order of Christ was the opening up of Africa to Europe[14].

In the life and struggle of great souls like Mahatma Gandhi or South Africa's Albert Luthuli are also seen the qualities of the servant leader, but there are many thousands of people working quietly and unknown in the squatter camps and poor villages of the world who have the qualities of love and dedication of the servant-leader. Whilst living under the most terrible conditions, they are still able to inspire and uplift their people.

Recognition

What can we do to develop, or rather how can we recognise the attributes of servant-leaders for the further growth of a spirit-centred, socially healthy, transnational culture if that is considered as the way, or a way, forward? Robert Greenleaf has suggested that a) more servants should become leaders and b) more people should follow servant-leaders. Most important is the quality mentioned in the beginning of this essay that the servant-leader will make sure that other people's highest priority needs are being met. What also are the effects of the servant-leader? Are they followers whilst being served, becoming healthier, wiser, freer, more autonomous, and become servants in turn? What also, is the effect upon the most disadvantaged in society?

What guarantees service! The servant-leader will more naturally persevere and redefine the hypothesis. The servant-leader will tend to listen; first to accept and empathise, and never reject. The servant-leader, according to Robert Greenleaf, needs to develop "a sense for the unknowable and foresee the unforeseeable"[15]; and inspires, never instructs.

The Servant Leader In South Africa

When we consider the world situation as it is today with its social degeneration, economic uncertainty and ecological danger signs, it seems that not only for South Africa, but for all nations, there is really no choice as to whether change is optional; the development of an entirely new culture based upon caring, a culture that enhances brotherhood between peoples, a culture that emulates 'Ubuntu,' a culture that manifests Rudolf Steiner's fundamental social law —

> The healthy social life is found when in the mirror of each human soul, the whole community finds its reflection and, when in the community, the virtue of each single one is living

— is required. Only a new and fundamentally different culture to the current materialist one is the only possibility for humanity to avoid further catastrophes.

However, what steps can be taken to bring such changes about? Stephen Covey, Morris Berman, Fritjof Capra and Rudolf Steiner are among many leaders who have given insights to the qualities and processes to be adopted. Two thousand years ago John the Baptist heralded the appearance of the Christ when he cried, "Metanoia! — Change your thinking, change your values."

Principle centred leadership can be developed and encouraged within our communities through vehicles like the civics. This could help the beginning of shifting human values from the current ownership of 'things' as a basis for inner and outer security to the honouring of human relationships with dignity. Through involvement in local government in a manner in which the citizens experience real ownership plus the understanding and acceptance of personal responsibility for our work and the earth, a new and healthy community life could be born. "When community is created, everyone is a leader and everyone is a follower. The corporation becomes a collective lifelong learning organisation."[16] (Gozdz 1993).

The wonderful effects that can come about through the change in the way in which people relate to each other in a caring community, has been beautifully portrayed in the story of the Rabbi's gift, related at the beginning of Scott Peck's book "The Different Drum", [17] in which a group of ageing monks in a dwindling order find a new beginning for their community when they find the secret of renewed respect for each other and for themselves when they awaken to the spirituality in each other.

South Africa however, is in a different situation than the old European countries who have so much tradition and history behind them that the thought of change seems almost impossible. Here in the South we have begun to build a new society with the political revolution that has now taken place. Our next step is to build a new economy with new ideas. The old methods will just not be able to support a community of 42 million people on the labour of only 6 million, but in order to do that, the fundamental basis of our culture has to change. We have to have a new education to meet the new situation. Children cannot eat their matric certificates, neither can our universities survive financially by having to employ a much larger staff and care for larger faculties than are really necessary just because the method of accepting new students results in very high intakes, followed soon after by a very high failure and dropout rate. We currently face academic absurdity when culturally and consciously unprepared university students go on the rampage, destroying property and disrupting classes demanding "pass one, pass all!"

It seems that we stand on a threshold between the inevitable collapse of the old culture of restriction (apartheid was fuelled by what Stephen Covey calls "a scarcity mentality") and a very new intended culture of sharing and caring. We have now a president in whom the qualities and virtues of servant-leadership are being demonstrated. Nelson Mandela is recognised not only as South Africa's leader, but as one of the great moral leaders of the world. President Mandela's courage not to compromise kept him in prison years longer than was envisaged. His numerous actions like his refusal to sign the scientific accord agreement in Mozambique in August 1994, whereas all other African heads of state had signed, until he had consulted with South African scientists, all go to show that here is a man truly dedicated

161

to serve his people by his spirit of inclusivity.

Let us hope that Nelson Mandela has suffered on our behalf and that we do not have to spend 27 years in a prison of our old thinking punished by the consequences of selfishness whilst our children bear the pain of spiritual famine in a world that could offer so much. May we have the courage to recognise the educational gifts and consciousness of the Rudolf Steiners, Peter Senges Stephen Coveys, and Robert Greenleafs, together with other truly free thinkers, educationalists and scientists who can give us the tools for personal and cultural transformation. May the inspiration of Nelson Mandela light the path ahead for a new spirit of construction and development, not just of South Africa, but of the world.

BIBLIOGRAPHY

1   Robert K. Greenleaf 1991: *The Servant as Leader*. The Robert K. Greenleaf Centre.
2   *Time Magazine* November 1994.
3   Laurens van der Post. *A Walk With A White Bushman*.1986. Chatto and Windus.
4   Alvin Toffler. *The Third Wave*. 1980. New York: Morrow.
5   Robert K. Greenleaf 1991.*The Servant as Leader*.
6   Stephen Covey.1989. *The Seven Habits of Highly Effective People*. New York: Simon & Schuster.
7   New Paradigms. October 1994. Newsletter of the Third Way Society.
8   Stephen Covey. 1992. *Principle-Centred Leadership*. New York.Simon & Schuster.
9   Fred Blum. The Scott Bader Commonwealth.
10 New Paradigms. October 1994.
11 Anita Roddick. 1992. Harper & Collins.
12 Harrison Owen. 1990. *Leadership Is*. Abbott Publishers.
13 Harrison Owen. 1992. *Riding the Tiger*. Abbott Publishers.
14 Robert Silverberg. 1972. *The Realm of Prester John*. Doubleday & Co.

15 Robert K Greenleaf. 1991. *The Servant as Leader.*

16 H.B. Maynard Jr. & Susan E. Mehrtens. 1993. *The Fourth Wave.* Berrett-Koehler Publishers.

17 M.Scott Peck. 1978. *The Different Drum.* Simon & Schuster.

Chapter 11

Mobilisation, Mobocracy or Mobile

Waldorf Education in Post-Apartheid South Africa

Brien Masters

IT OFTEN COMES AS A SHOCK when someone hears for the first time that the Jordan Valley in Israel is still 'on the move' — measurably, however slightly. This is not just a matter of erosion by wind or waves, which even though such features are found in various places across the world on a vast scale, could still be said to be 'surface phenomena' — cosmetic (though the word is not used lightly) rather than fundamental. I am not suggesting that the realisation that a whole valley the length and breadth of the Jordan is actually moving causes the sort of sudden shock as occasioned, say, by an earthquake of the dimension that was suffered in Japan in January, 1995, which brought about so much human tragedy, or other such seismatic phenomena not uncommon on the Pacific Rim. The latter may engender fear on the one hand and compassion on the other. Whereas reaction to the former (the Jordan Valley movement) is perhaps closer to awe. This awe springs from the fact that what we normally take for granted as static — the physical world — defies us by moving, shakes our very concept of the stability and dependability of firm earth.

Culture, and more especially civilisation, is the reverse. There, we expect change, movement, development, strong contrasts ('culture shocks') etc. On the whole, our expectations are fulfilled; occasionally they are fulfilled overwhelmingly, and this is essentially what the world experienced in everything that accelerated towards the inclusion of the Voices of Africa in the post-Apartheid Government — though this is not intended as a political statement of any sort, but merely to symbolise a process of change. For those 'outside' — even, as in my case, for a somewhat distant spectator — those events were remarkable by any standards. If one tried to live through them, as if inwardly accompanying those involved, then they were indeed awesome.

The Jordan Valley, deep below sea level, lies towards the northern extremity of the great African rift which zigzags its way from North to South, taking in the route of the water-course currently being proposed by the King of Jordan (to link the Red and the Dead Seas), the Gulf of Aqaba and the Red Sea itself, the line of great lakes through Ethiopia, Kenya, Malawi and Tanzania 'down' to Mozambique. At the foot of this rift — with its East-West cross, one arm extending westwards into the Mediterranean and the other eastwards into the Euphrates Valley and the Persian Gulf, or further north into its northern branch through the Caspian Sea — stands South Africa. In fact, a legendary image places South Africa at the foot of the "world cross." And allied to that image, one might think of Table Mountain, dominating the Cape with the remarkably flat top that gives it its name, as the footstool of that cross.

It was the artists of Northern Europe who depicted, with particularly poignant effect, the emotional — even passionate — response of the followers of Jesus of Nazareth to the events of the 'Passion.' One could cite the trance-like agony of the Mother of Jesus, in Grunewald's Isenheim altarpiece, as she stands below the figure whose writhing hands and almost clenched fingers painfully and eloquently reveal what the crucifixion had caused to pass through her soul and spirit; or the awe-ful, hand-wringing gesture of irrevocability of John the Disciple as he kneels at the foot of the cross, against a background of ominously tense green, in the 'small' crucifixion in Washington by the same painter. Or again, the rage, verging paradoxically on rapture, of those who mock the Christ figure in Grunewald's painting in the Munich Alte Pinakothek collection. These are particularly telling examples from the hand of one artist alone. Other painters, Hieronymous Bosch for instance, could equally well be called to give similar testimony. Moreover (though this will be more fully dealt with later) these artists were at work at the self-same time that Portuguese eyes were first to behold Table Mountain.

It cannot be so easy for 20th century land-lubbers to realise what went on inside those sailors, as they stood on the decks of their doughty lateen-rigged caravels, weeks of toil at sea having passed since they embarked at Sargres. But perhaps the imagination that we are 'carrying,' of the footstool of the world cross, can bring us some distance towards that realisation.

As tears of rage and sorrow variously filled the eyes of the bystanders as they stood on the hill of Golgotha (the place of the skull), so Table Mountain is often the scene of either violent weather (The Cape of Storms was how white man first referred to it) or topped with billowing white clouds which tumble northwards, bearing rain to the hinterland of the Cape, which is blessed with one of the most beautifully rich flora on the face of the whole globe. When we experience spring in the Cape, we might well be reminded of the atmosphere on the first Easter morning, the stone from the sepulchre rolled away, and of the Magdalen in the garden, weeping at the supposed loss of her Lord and Master (Rabboni), "turning herself" at the sound of her name. We may imagine her at that moment moving from spiritual darkness into a new state of consciousness — a new form of Paradise, not simply 'coming full circle,' but spirally exalted through the triumph over death that had been enacted for all time and for all humanity, starting three days before, on Good Friday.

Recalling and providing commentary on the scene at the foot of the Cross on Golgotha, are two of the most majestic bars of music ever written: they are in Bach's immortal The St. Matthew Passion, at the point where the choir sings the words "Truly this was the Son of God." The means by which the composer achieves this seem straightforward enough to the analytical mind: a small handful of basic chords, uncomplicated part writing, smooth step-wise motion in the melodic contours... all testimony to the fact that genius does not require the abstruse or the eccentric to express itself. However, the majesty of this moment, at which the composer voices recognition of who Jesus of Nazareth actually was, has been preceded by unparalleled musical turbulence: "The veil of the temple was rent in twain...", "The earth did quake; the rocks were rent..." So much so that it could be maintained that it is through the foregoing turbulence that the music is lifted to its heights of inimitable and unrivalled sublimity.

In the April elections of 1994, the whole world standing by apprehensively saw the veil of South Africa's apartheid "rent in twain." Not unexpectedly, much social upheaval still troubles the land, but there is no doubt that a new dawn has broken. It was as if Mandela's path, which led towards and enabled the combating of racial injustice, became illuminated by the light that had already been kindled by figures such as Ghandi in the east and Martin Luther King in the West, to name only two of the most prominent. The biographies of Ghandi (q.v. his suffering at the hands of racism in the first-class train compartment) and of Martin Luther King (whose mission was prompted by the famous bus incident) can both be read as journeys of peace, surrounded by turbulence, though they are by no means parallel in detail.

Still less parallel is Nelson Mandela's journey; outwardly the

168

contrasts are obvious — stark at times. From the moment Ghandi, as a young barrister, stepped onto South African soil, in 1893 — interestingly enough exactly a century plus one year earlier than the electoral event that affirmed the new South Africa — he fought for the legal rights of the relatively large Indian population, principally in the Durban area. Idiosyncratically, the first impact there was the dispute in court with the Magistrate over his turban, the incident being lapped up by the press, where he was branded as an "unwelcome visitor." But this did not put Ghandi off his stroke: with characteristic diplomacy he succeeded in getting the case he was concerned with satisfactorily settled out of court. "My joy was boundless," he stated, "I had learnt to find out the better side of human nature and to enter men's hearts."

This comes across as something of a hallmark in Ghandi's biography: even on a professional level, his genius was able to find the distinct point of compromise (in hundreds of cases, as it turned out, during his twenty years of practice as a lawyer). Which compromise may perhaps be interpreted as the point at which conflict could adjust itself to find the 'balance' that was acceptable and satisfactory to both sides. That Ghandi was unswervingly faithful to this principle may be confirmed by identifying it in all the minor and major incidents that formed part of and surrounded the remarkable progress of his life. Even when his life was brought to an abrupt and tragic end, after British rule had been withdrawn from India and he was playing the part of the peacemaker in the disputes that had broken out in the internal affairs of the country, his thoughts and prayers included the plight of minorities elsewhere in the world, that of the Indians in Natal being foremost amongst them.

It is obviously too early to look for hallmarks in Mandela's life or to say with certainty what his path might be; but one thing is clear: "the better side of human nature" seems to have prevailed to an unprecedented extent both in international and in State affairs leading up to the elections, despite the unease and uncertainty that rumbled threateningly below the surface in the months prior. The long polling queues on election day, with their painfully slow yet movingly good-natured progress, came over as being in inverse proportion to the astonishing rate of advance in human relationships. In this case, De Klerk was repeatedly pictured, at least by the European media, as standing at Mandela's side — initially it was vice versa — participating in the political course of events.

Of course, as has been pointed out, nothing remains at rest in civilization. Particularly is this true of politics. (Were it otherwise, the press would look very different and the media would have to find a whole catalogue of different tunes to play.) Upset the balance of power and the oscillations resulting from that upset are bound to continue, even reaching violent proportions. And it is necessary to bear in mind in South Africa's case that, although at face value it was a matter of one person handing on the baton to one other, this is a huge (even, perhaps, hugely distorted) simplification of the underlying reality.

In any political situation, we are not dealing with a balance such as that found in the market place — even if the provision of governance is principally a two-party system. A more exact metaphor would be that of a mobile: suspended from a pivotal point, as is a pair of scales, but, unlike scales, having umpteen subsidiary strings and weights which, when the mobile is still, settle into a particular patterns But when a breath of wind blows, or the mobile is disturbed by convectional currents circulating in the room, the whole pattern becomes mobile. Or, still more pertinent perhaps, if a weight is suddenly added or removed, the pattern becomes turbulent, and everything is affected. Thus, even as one writes, or even thinks about any given political situation — an agreement here or a riot there; a resignation here or a promotion there; an innovation here, a resistance there; outspokenness at one moment, back-room manoeuvring at another; negotiation at one point, force and bloodshed somewhere else, etc. — all the mobile, however slightly or strongly, in all 13 language-groups, in all political parties, in all segments of society, has to adjust. We may look to such a cause when a school changes the proportion of blacks to whites on its roll call; when a face that was once prominent, is no longer seen; a name once on all lips, becomes very little heard of; a party once in power and taking the political initiative finds itself roller-coasting and having to negotiate unaccustomed encumbrances; or when a farmer loses his labourers who have gone off to seek (not their fortunes) but their pensions ....

But in all this, it is perhaps worthwhile to recall that as the mask of apartheid was being torn aside, it revealed the smile of genuine friendship, however fleeting that smile might now appear to have been. It was without doubt a moment, on that April day, for the rest of the world to look within, to awaken in self-knowledge to the fact that, although the symptom had surfaced most strongly in South Africa, the underlying social illness of apartheid had been widespread, in a variety of ethnic settings across the globe, sanctions or no. (The very coming into common usage of an expression such as 'ethnic cleansing' — an expression which, astonishingly and for many repulsively, is being digested, it seems without pain, into the language where it now frequently turns up without inverted commas — should serve as sufficient reminder of the extent of the malady here being alluded to.)

Already in the years leading up to this moment of historic conscience, the Waldorf schools in South Africa had done a certain amount to bring members of the different ethnic communities together, side by side. Though at times more of a homoeopathic symbol of integration than anything to be numerically proud of, it was still an achievement that black, white and coloured children sat together under one roof. That good work, if one looks at the patchwork quilt of South African Waldorf education as a whole, goes on. Now, however, in their struggle with the questions: How can the confluence of rich cultural diversity from the past be effected? and: How can the spirit of a people becoming united evolve further into the future? the longer established schools — in Johannesburg, Durban, Pretoria and the two in the Cape — are joined by the courageous and widely acclaimed efforts of the Waldorf initiatives in the townships, and also by The Rudolf Steiner Centre for Teacher Education and The Novalis Institute. Through such efforts, Waldorf is being brought to a wider population than ever before, who are welcoming it with open arms

171

and rare enthusiasm. Hand-clasps of collegiate friendship are beginning to close the gaping rift of past centuries, following the example
of the political leaders.

At this juncture it would be well to recall 'one' of the seven last
words that rang out close on 2000 years ago from the Cross of Golgotha: "Woman behold thy son..." In contemplating these, we become aware that the two sorrowing figures at the foot of the cross
(John the disciple and Mary the mother of Jesus) to whom the words
were addressed were not, as the words might suggest at first hearing,
related through family. That is to say, from the Cross, two Jews are
addressed — and it is good to remind ourselves from time to time
that the spirit of Christianity first 'incarnated' into Jewish blood —
as "mother" and "son," despite the fact that they were unrelated and
that family was (and still is) an extremely important factor in the
social structure of Judaic life. Here was something cutting right across
the blood-tie — a new social signature-tune, the first phrase of which
was heard at the marriage that was celebrated in the Canaan district
of Galilee, continuing to sound through that acme of all parables The
Good Samaritan, to its crescendo which culminates at this point. In
terms of human relationships, it was the dawn of a new age.

Space does not allow us here to follow the progress of that dawn
through the ages. Not that progress is always synonymous with ease:
history is teeming with the corpses of Romeos and Juliets. At surface,
Shakespeare's play on the theme is a tragedy about thwarted lovers;
beneath, it offers a mirror in which society can look at its inability
to cross over the boundary of blood-relationships. Yet at the end of
the play, prompted by the heart-rending loss — sacrifice — of Romeo
and Juliet, the two families do 'make it up,' promising a more ami-
cable future. Even so, it is not difficult to admit that we still have a
long way to go. Moreover, that long way is not made easier by the
fact that, as the ego becomes a stronger and stronger entity, it will
consequently become subject to more and more temptation to egotism,
which in turn pushes beyond reach the altruism of "Mother behold
thy son." Not that we would want to escape: for in essence, this is
the story of the world. And in this respect the new South Africa has

set up a splendid Camp One, in readiness for the Everest that lies ahead.

But this is not the only peak that soars upwards in the landscape of the dawn that we are looking at, not the only challenge along the ego's ascent to freedom. To begin with, for centuries, soul and spirit featured in all aspects of life within that dawn. In whatever part of the spectrum of human thinking, the soul-spiritual dimension of life still formed of the world outlook of peoples through many changes of culture.

Until when? It is at the height of the Renaissance that the roots of a new way of thinking can be discovered: the mechanistic view of the human being and of the whole of creation. That is to say the confining of knowledge to that which can be derived from a purely sensorial (empirically ordered, examinable, analysable) view of the world and, as its corollary, the exclusion from that view, by a mate-rialistic mode of thinking, of all that is metaphysical. Hamlet, another of Shakespeare's characters, is one of the first to give dramatic voice to what this step meant. It is as if humanity were being thrust all over again out of its paradisal garden, in which the soul-spiritual had been sovereign, into a world of toil and sweat in which the toil only took account of and was directed exclusively towards earthly forces and the sweat was regarded merely as a chemical process from a being — homo sapiens — that was gradually atrophying towards a kind of Cartesian spectre: I excrete, therefore I am.

It was Steiner's view that this descent in human development was essential for the emancipation that is inherent in what we refer to as 'freedom.' Indeed, until that point of nadir had been reached, a self-directed ascent could not begin. It is therefore of great signifi-cance that the age of changed thinking is simultaneous with the age that, through changed thinking, began to plunge humanity into mate-rialism, with the impulse to set sail, leaving familiar shores behind, and discover the new. In the West was the New World. In Africa was what we might call, in the present context, the search for the New Kingdom. The Spanish quest for gold (Westward) has often been presented as counterbalanced by the quest of Portugal. Eastwards,

173

yes; but via the Cape.

Thus it was that on Christmas Day 1497, at the dawn of the age of discovery, Vasco da Gama and his Portuguese sailors gave the Terra do Natal its name. That event's half millenium is about to be celebrated.

There is much to be found in the fifteenth century, in the log books of what has been described as Portuguese Maritime Enterprise, that one can sense re-surfacing in the voyage that South Africa is disposed towards 'today'. Half a dozen examples spring to mind :

(i) The starting point of this particular chapter of history can essentially be traced to the audacity with which King John of Portugal (before he became king) took the law into his own hands to cleanse the Dukedom of corruption. It was not, by all accounts, prompted by blood connections (as were many internecine feuds) but by force of pure moral integrity. Significantly, his reign (1385–1433) straddled the year which is usually associated with the birth of the Consciousness Soul. Moreover, the victory at Queta, prior to which John's four sons were knighted by their mother as she lay on her deathbed, was in that very year: 1415. Though moral integrity is not something that is handed on genetically, in the spirit of Queen Philippa was surely inscribed something of her father's spirit when he, John of Gaunt, upbraided the too hedonistically inclined young Richard II of England.

(ii) Often overlooked in the history of the Portuguese crusade (for such the period of discovery under consideration has often been classified) is the 16 year lull of (1418–1434), when success seemed to languish in the doldrums, but throughout which Henry the Navigator persevered with unflagging inner certainty and single-mindedness.

(iii) The purely spiritual/cultural link with England which was achieved can be seen symbolised best, perhaps, through Henry's being dubbed Knight of the Order of the Garter in 1442, fascinatingly enough, by his namesake Henry VI of England. Both were scholars. Henry VI's destiny thrust the crown of kingship upon him, whereas in the Portuguese Henry's case, he was liberated from this through being the third son. Though the outer ramifications of this may be difficult to detect, let alone assess, the special link between England and Portugal (two consciousness soul countries, it could be argued) was even remarked upon by Winston Churchill, speaking as recently as 1943 concerning the "Use of Facilities in the Azores," as something that was without precedent in world history. Churchill, statesman that he was, cited no fewer than ten treaties, dating back to 1373, to give emphasis to his point. It would be naïve to suggest that that mutual regard at a formal international level has been so transmuted that it has become a saving grace in the 'present' events of 1994, yet might its continuance not be credited with having given those events at least a 'fair wind'? Be that as it may, the indisputable fact remains that something is at work in South Africa — the causes of which will presumably become discernible as time goes on — something that did not formerly appear to be so readily available, for instance, in the case of Zimbabwe.

(iv) There is the remarkable example of what Damiao Peres described in 1960 (on the 500th anniversary of the death of Prince Henry) as an "absolute novelty in the history of the world": he was referring to Diogo Cao's penetration into the interior of Africa in 1489, entering to begin with through the estuary of the Zaire, and establishing *"cordial civilised relations* [my italics] between a European people" and a number of indigenous tribes.

(v) Then there was the division of land deemed to be necessary at the Treaty of Tordesillas in 1494, yet all ultimately under the same Christian ensign — in those days, that of Rome, of course.

(vi) There was the essentially unsung sacrifice of Fernando (Henry's brother) who died in captivity 'for the cause' — a named martyr, who could also be taken as representative for many a 'warrior' still to this day unknown.

(vii) Finally we return to Henry and the great example he set in giving his all (and more in terms of outer wealth!), entirely for the future; for at his death (13 November 1460) his plans were still in many ways still only in embryo.

There is no need, within the limits of the present essay, to spell out all the 'symptomatic' connections between the above and the phase of history through which we are presently navigating. Nevertheless it is pertinent to ask: Whither were those sailors from Portugal really bound? Why call it a "crusade"? In his article *Prester John and the Voyages of Discovery'* (included in this volume) Ralph Shepherd states that South Africa was discovered by those "en route to Prester John." He asserts that the Order that supported the exploration was founded on the rock of Johannine Christianity.

To what extent the Prester John saga is fact or fiction, legendary or 'legitimate', real or imaginary, we can leave on one side for the present. For in some ways, irrespective of which side of the empirical fence it falls on, the kingdom of Prester John is one of the most truly Christian kingdoms ever envisaged (i.e. where mere labels of Christianity count for nothing). One wonders whether the search for it is not somehow parallel to the search for the buried treasure in that comparatively well-known story, in which the sons of a dying father were bequeathed land, in which supposed treasure lay somewhere hidden as their heritage. The story unveils how their 'treasure hunt' (which had the effect of absolutely regular and conscientiously thorough ploughing) did in fact yield the treasure: not a chest of gold coins, however, but unfailingly abundant harvests. In a similar way one could well imagine the kingdom of Prester John coming into being wherever the search for it takes place in all earnestness, i.e. not through outer voyages but through those of inner sincerity and striving, brotherhood and service. This would entail the steady, person-to-person cultivation of a new social ethic, something along the lines of what is encapsulated in Rudolf Steiner's challenging yet insightful

"The more that people are segregated, the less will it be possible for higher beings to descend to the human realm. [But] the more that connections are formed — the feeling for community created out of free will — the more will it be possible for higher beings to descend, [to work like a kind of new group soul] in full harmony with human liberty and individuality."

But however much, and however transliterated, such a social ethic were to be emblazoned from the balcony of Government House — and clearly a strong element of being seen to be integrated as well as having an up-front policy of integration is indispensable in the leadership of the country — one could hardly expect the Kingdom here referred to as 'Prester John' really to be discovered and ultimately realised unless the same ethic were cultivated in the warm-hearted humanness of factory and farmstead, chapel and lecture-hall, box-office and taxi-rank. Failing this, the reality that we have to contend with will be one thing, and Prester John will remain something on paper which, however well set out or beautifully illustrated and bound that paper may be, will collect the same dust on its bookshelf as its neighbour volumes.

It is recorded that a woman once came to Ghandi not with a political axe to grind but with a simple mother's request: Would he please tell her son to stop eating sugar! Ghandi acquiesced, telling the woman to send her son to him in three months' time, whereupon he did as she had requested. Thankful, yet puzzled after the event, the woman asked: "But why the three months delay?" He looked at her with the compassion and wisdom that few but he were able to impart: "First I had to give up sugar myself."

Hence, perhaps we may be permitted to interpret, without being guilty of transmogrifying: Where "two or three" travel earnestly together and with mutual goodwill, in search of The Kingdom, there it shall arise, in their midst.

Certainly one senses that, among the voyagers of the New South Africa, there are those with new purpose and initiative who have embarked once again for the 'shores' of such a kingdom and who hold such an ethic. The task of undertaking the journey is awesome, but at the same time pivotal for the future and immensely inspiring.

There will be those who hold that as yet there is no such thing as post-apartheid South Africa, that all the benefits that can accrue from integration are coming too slowly. The term is used here, as has been demonstrated above, purely to indicate the mind-stretching potential of the post-1994-election era. Of course, segregation must be on the way out more quickly than the imperceptible movement of a Jordan Valley. But equally unsatisfactory — leaving their own trails of destruction — are earthquakes in the socio-political life. A pace needs to be found that lies somewhere between the grinding tank-crawl of an army being mobilized and the outbursts in which mobocracy smashes positive planning and genuine care into smithereens. Each individual or group (at whatever hierarchical level) needs to consider as much as possible the effect on the total movement of the 'mobile' when they act.

In a British Museum (London) catalogue of 1960, Henry the Navigator was once summed up as one who had "a place both in the dying age of chivalry and in the opening age of scientific enquiry." This seems to be saying that we are dealing with an individuality who was a 'Prince' in two worlds: the earthly and the heavenly. One can recognise in this dual-worldliness, if one may coin such an expression, the seal of modern Rosicrucianism.

Now, however, it is mostly necessary to view the situation from the other end of the telescope i.e. as not perhaps a dying scientific age (in the sense of receding: we cannot expect science to 'turn up its toes'; nor would we wish it), but one in which it has become necessary, now that science has led humanity towards a certain threshold, to cultivate, earthly, well-grounded qualities, alongside those of that spirit which is seeking a fully contemporary renewal.

One can only earnestly wish all who are concerned in such renewal, in all aspects of society in the new South Africa — and especially, in the context of the present publication, all those involved in the Waldorf movement there — God's speed and sails filled with the fair winds of Hope, Faith and Love when rounding the Cape of Storms.

Chapter 12

Angels, Tribalism and the Coming Culture

From a Consciousness of Dependency to the Consciousness of Interdependency :

The Journey from Group Consciousness to the New Brotherhood

— *Ralph Shepherd* —

T HE HISTORY OF THE EVOLUTION of human conscious-
ness, has been exhaustively researched from every conceivable point
of view and from every possible aspect. However, in order for us to
explore the theme of this essay, we will have to give some considera-

tion to the development in human consciousness reflected in history, and the effects that these changes have had upon human community life through the ages from a possible new perspective.

It seems that the further we look back on the development of human consciousness, the less we find the expression of human individuality[1] and the greater we find the phenomena of a group or community consciousness. Even today in Africa and elsewhere in the developing world it is still possible to find small communities in which group consciousness — a consciousness in which human beings exhibit no independent existence from the tribe or clan, a consciousness which forces subservience of the individual to the group — still remains as the basis of community life. In the old USSR the Bolsheviks attempted to enforce this form of community consciousness on the peoples of Russia. Neither the sociological understanding or the economic philosophy of Marxist-Leninism, had any lasting reality for the Eastern Bloc countries. Now (1995), we witness the consequences of a failed social experiment six years after the collapse of Russian Communism, but we are also witnessing the inability of Western Capitalism to replace the old order. Something entirely new, a different social and economic paradigm needs to replace Western Capitalism and Communism both of which are the fruits of Western Materialism expressed through dry intellectualism in which the reality of the spirit is denied.

With the decline of group or collective domination over the individual in society, we are also witnessing the sharp rise in human independence concurrent with the rise in anti-social activities such as crime and violence. As we become more individuated the less we express the need for community or so it seems. If that is the case, then the War of All against All described in the last book in the Bible, will soon be upon us. The decline in social order and the alarming rise in violent crime world-wide seems to indicate that we human beings are generally heading in the direction referred to in the book of Revelation. The social future of humankind or even the future of humankind itself seems grim indeed, unless a new social awareness together with a new social technology can be developed and introduced to human society before we reach the point of total collapse.

The industro-technology that has given our age the possibility for human beings to become materially self sufficient, has also facilitated the rise of anti-social forces. In pre-industrial cultures, human interaction within community was a material necessity for the provision of food and shelter. Co-operation between people and thereby community involvement was fundamental to staying alive. Today, with the aid of the telephone and computer together with the other marvels of modern technology we can live our lives without direct human interaction and live in a semblance of self sufficiency. Fortunately the development away from group consciousness does not stop at the independence of each individual from each other but is itself a state in the process of growth towards interdependence, that condition of consciousness in which strong individualism consciously contributes towards the welfare of the community at large.

We can now observe in history and in modern societies the great journey of human consciousness from a group community consciousness of dependency, to a selfish independence in which individuals feel that they no longer need the support of a community, followed by a state of interdependence or co-operative awareness[2]. This state of co-operative awareness in which self conscious individuals freely concern themselves with the needs of their fellow human beings as expressed in the first Christian community, appears to be the state that, in recent times, has been increasingly sought after by socially concerned individuals and groups. In Israel we witnessed the rise and growth of the kibbutzim in the nineteen forties whilst the hippie movement of the 1960s saw the advent of the 'commune.'

One movement that came into being in the late 1930s to consciously create communities that were not based upon national or tribal group consciousness but upon free spiritual values, was the international Camphill Movement. Inspired by the teachings of Dr Rudolf Steiner, the founders of the Camphill Movement decided that as they were creating a community 'outside' society at large, that they would take one of society's problems with them.

Named after the village in north Scotland in which it was founded,

Camphill took upon itself the care of the mentally disabled. Today, Camphill villages are established all over the world. There are three such villages in South Africa and one in Botswana serving approximately 270 handicapped adults with approximately 120 co-workers. The Camphill villages contain workshops, craft centres and bio-dynamic farms. The Hemel and Aarde Camphill village at Hermanus in the Western Cape also has its own school. Not only do these villages and farms produce healthy products for their own consumption, they also produce enough to sell on the open market. Co-workers in Camphill consciously strive for social interdependence in their community. Camphill is one of the first communities that strives to live in a manner that harmonises the needs of the community with the needs of the individual member.

Healthy social interdependence is also beginning to emerge in modern business houses. The Scott Bader Commonwealth and The Body Shop in England, and Semco in Brazil (see background to these companies in the essay on *The Servant Leader* in this anthology) in which circular management has replaced pyramid management are three such examples. In these organisations, every staff member feels fully responsible for the whole organisation. In Semco and Scott Bader, employees are also shareholders in their own right. However, this new paradigm of conscious co-operative awareness is still only a glimmer on the horizon in the evolution of human consciousness. Unfortunately, all we seem to see on the television news programmes, are the negative effects of tribal or group consciousness manifesting in mob violence and brutality on the one side, and the crass selfishness of egotism manifesting in self enrichment — at the expense of the community at large — on the other.

Through a new understanding or insight into community living such as striven for by Dr M Scott Peck in his bestselling book *A Different Drum* and Dr Rudolf Steiner's *Threefold Commonwealth* (which is the basis for the Camphill Movement's community life), is showing by example how healthy interdependence can be attempted. Both Scott Peck and Steiner have developed techniques to assist in the development of particular social skills for the furthering of healthy

182

social interaction, one in which the needs of the individual and of the community at large can be mutually satisfied and enhanced.

In South Africa, although burdened by alarmingly high rates of violence and crime and an economy too small to bring relief to all her citizens living below the bread line, new social forms are being sought in all spheres of our society. Invitations to all South Africans through the press by the Government of National Unity, to contribute to the formation of a new constitution; a constitution based upon full community participation. In this gesture of participation can be seen the possiblility of a new social communion if the government is courageous enough to adopt new thoughts. Only time will show the success or failure of South Africans to respond positively to this challenge and create a new society. However, goodwill alone is not sufficient to create a new society, new and exciting social forms that go beyond the confines of the paradigms of the existing social order, have also to be introduced.

Current methods of social restructuring and intervention based upon reductionist thinking have achieved little in dealing with today's economic and social problems. For all our institutions of learning, and vast sums spent on research, the world socially, economically and ecologically is in a worse state than ever before. For example, in drug rehabilitation centres world wide, hundreds of millions are spent assisting drug addicts to overcome their dependency yet we see a more than a 90% relapse rate! Are our institutions incapable of real healing, or are our methods of research so fundamentally wrong that we will never find answers to our current ills? Are the two primary factors in current world economics, armaments sales and illegal drug sales,[3] controlling the social life of humanity? — or are they the effects of a sick organism? Arms and drugs are more like flies around garbage. The flies don't create the garbage: we have. In like manner, the illnesses of our social life have created the conditions in which weapons of war and illicit drugs have become the first two major factors in our global economics.

How can we develop new methods of social research to understand our current social crisis? We cannot carry on investigating the problems of the world using reductionist thinking. As Einstein has said, "You can't use the same thinking that created the problems in the first place!" Again the question is, do we have the courage — courage to go beyond the material limitations of Positivism, beyond the boundaries of knowledge set by Kant[4] and into the new realms of research opened up by Johann Wolfgang von Goethe[5] and explored and developed further by Rudolf Steiner[6,7] in the early part of this century? Since Steiner's time, other scientists[8] have developed the courage to cross inner thresholds or boundaries necessary for this new approach to research.

Over the past four hundred years Cartesian-Kantian thinking or epistemology and the accompanying philosophy of Positivism have so penetrated our conception and perception of the world, that it is almost impossible to imagine any other kind beyond or interpenetrating the physical world we know. The only existential reference that we have left to us of other worlds are the inner dimensions of our imagination and our world of dreams both of which defy logic and quantification; yet they exist as common experiences for every human being. Flashes of inspiration and intuition are also experiences belonging to an unquantifiable reality.

In contrast, the 'inner' realm opened up to scientific research by Rudolf Steiner[9] introduces us to a universe in which mythology and wonder once again have a place in our souls as a living reality. A universe in which self-conscious beings beyond the human state have their existence. Beings with abilities and consciousness beyond that developed so far by mankind, beings now only referred to in myths and fairy tales. A universe where human souls find their true home between death and a new life on earth[10] and where, for a while, are removed from the struggle with the deterioration and pain of our physical bodies wrought by the passage of time and the natural world around us.

Partly because of our education springing out of our western materialistic culture, it appears almost impossible for modern humanity to consider realms other than the physical world of the five senses. Yet the rise in the New Age movement can be seen as a yearning of the human soul to be re-connected to the divine. Unfortunately, the New Age movement is seen generally as an escape from responsibility and not the inclusion of a higher reality.

The growing awareness of 'Systems Thinking' in which holism is expounded as the new epistemology from which we may find the way to a new consciousness, demands that we are 'inclusive' in our contemplation of the world , and that means the invisible realms as well! Systems thinking without the total reality, which currently excludes the spiritual or divine world, is only restructured or disguised Positivism. It is in this area that courage needs to be developed, a courage that enables the traveller or spiritual scientist, to enter inner dimensions whilst maintaining full consciousness. This approach to spiritual investigation stands in direct contrast to what today is referred to in the New Age movement as "channelling" in which messages, instructions and other communications are supposedly channelled through a medium who remains unconscious of the realm from which these communications come. This process does not allow for any conscious research and therefore remains questionable against the light of a developing consciousness.

One experience for consideration that will help us to develop the courage to take inner journeys of discovery and which will also assist in understanding the existence of other beings in that realm of 'beingness' without a physical body, is a contemplation on the nature of our own physical body itself.

Each human being cares, protects and to a certain extent loves his or her own body, and it is also our body that is the basis for our current sense of reality, and also of our sense of physical permanency. Yet few realise that this body of ours is never more than seven years old. Buckminster Fuller often pointed out to his students that the average life span of a human cell was only two years! Yet our memory extends far beyond the time limitation of our body, which is continually in a state of change and becoming. We can be even more surprised by the further knowledge that between 70% and 80% of our body is water, and that the water aspect of our body changes completely every two weeks! The physical world no longer seems as secure as the inner

185

world of our thoughts and images when we consider the transience of our own body. Such thoughts help us consider or rather overcome the blocks brought about by our indoctrination in the Cartesian-Kantian mindsets towards new paradigms in consciousness, new paradigms in research.

Spiritual scientific investigation, (see Rudolf Steiner above) seems to be the best term to use for this new method of research in which the investigator becomes him or herself, the instrument of investigation, the microscope or telescope of the inner world. But like any instrument, it must be prepared and honed in order to be worthy of the investigator. A faulty telescope or microscope is of no use to the physical investigator, so to would an unprepared or untrained investigator be useless as a spiritual researcher. The preparation and training required have been described in detail[11] and are not the subject of this brief essay.

All technological scientific equipment and instruments in use today, are merely the extension of human faculties and senses. Research has revealed that the intentions and attitudes of the researchers have actual effects upon the research phenomenon itself.[12] As this is the case in physics, where the previous intent was 'objective' research, we now come to a new understanding that objectivity and subjectivity have to be combined into what can be termed as Goetheanistic observation after Goethe who developed this approach to scientific inquiry.[13] The nature of the investigator has — in natural science alone — become a part of the research equipment itself! It is easy to contemplate then, the idea of a 'spiritual researcher' being both instrument and investigator at the same time.

Before we continue with our consideration of community consciousness we have to look behind the external phenomena of human groupings to see what force (if any) draws people together or keeps them in separate camps. From where comes the power of attraction we call nationalism or group identity? What is the magnetism behind the John Bull of England or the Uncle Sam of the United States, images that once compelled men to "rally around the flag" and go off leaving family and home to fight a war? Today, we see the same

186

phenomena manifesting in Islamic and Christian fundamentalists. In South Africa, group binding power manifests in right and left-wing extremism and in the ongoing battle between the ANC and the IFP.

In times past, groups of human beings or communities were said to be held together by group or Folk Spirits: super-human, non-physical, beings whose task it was to guide and lead their communities. England has or had its Albion (or 'John Bull'), old Israel had its Jahwe or Jahova. What immense power once flowed from these super-human beings, and what caused their decline? How are new group spirits brought into being? These questions need consideration before we proceed with our study.

Reference has been made in other essays in this book to beings from beyond the physical threshold. Beings with self-awareness but with a much higher state of consciousness than is experienced by humankind today. Beings now only known only to us in mythology and in the world's great religions. Those beings whom we know as 'angels'[14] not only have a real existence in spirit realms, but history and observation (and revelation) have shown that they have an effect upon the physical world and human communities. They are members of those creative spiritual powers who hold the physical world together as well as interface with our human community's development.

Most religions describe, albeit from different points of view, the existence of a hierarchy of Celestial Beings between man and the Godhead whose tasks are to further the process of creation itself. Christian theology lists nine levels of angelic beings, and places them into three groups of three. The ranks of command in both the military and the church[15] were, until very recently, modelled on the ranking of the celestial heirarchies. The first group of three superhuman beings, the Angels, Archangels and Archai or Principalities, are described as being directly involved in the development of humankind. The second group of three, the Elohim, Dynameis and Kyriotetes are responsible for maintaining and ordering of the universe whilst the last group of three, the Thrones, Cherubim and Seraphim create the substance of worlds directly under the Trinity of the Godhead. The study of the Celestial Hierarchies has recently experienced a resurgence after almost five hundred years, with many books now appearing treating the subject with renewed interest.[16]

Crossing the threshold of the physical limits of perception brings humankind into contact with an entire aspect of creation that had become lost to our consciousness during the last four hundred years, yet it is out of this invisible world that the visible world has sprung. Systems thinking can only be truly based upon systems if the invisible worlds and its inhabitants are taken into consideration in its epistemology. Holistic thinking is not whole without the fullness of the created world and that must include the invisible realms as well. For this essay, we will consider only some aspects of the First Hierarchy, those Beings who are particularly and intimately concerned with our future development but who, in the highest sense of the word, do not interfere with our freedom.

The task of the Angel is described[17] as caring for the development of the individual human being through directing inspirations and imaginations that will help the individual towards his or her destiny. Again this is meant in the highest sense of the word and not the fulfilling of some earthly goal if the earthly one is at variance with the higher one. The spiritual goal is intended to enhance the 'be-ingness' of the individuality whereas most earthly goals are strivings after the possession or acquisition of something, whether that be money or status. Spiritual goals always take us beyond what we are. If our own strivings are in harmony with our own destiny determined before birth, then the process is joy-filled. If, on the other hand, our striving on earth is at variance with our spiritual goals, then the process could well be a painful one. The angels continually bring us the inspirations and also the conditions that lead us onwards and upwards.

The Archangel is concerned with the development of groups or communities of human beings yet with the same intent as the Angels — spiritual growth; whilst the Archai or Principalities are responsible for the development of humankind through time. In Esoteric Christianity, the Archai are also known as the Spirits of Time; they assist in our growth on a global basis through the great changes in world culture whereas the Archangels work with nations and other defined social groupings. The Archai bring about the conditions for a new consciousness through inspiring paradigm shifts in culture like the Renaissance or our technological culture. The Archangels develop the language or social pattern of a particular group or nation.[18]

However, not all the beings in the realms of spirit are beneficent in relation to the development of humankind as described by St.Paul[9]. We have then the responsibility to discern what impulses we will respond to, whether they harden our egotism or enhance our selfless individuation; help develop our community awareness or anti-social forces. "For we do not wrestle with flesh and blood, but against Principalities, against Powers, against the rulers of the darkness of this age, against spiritual hosts of wickedness in the heavenly places (realms)." [20]

In earlier times, before the development of individuation, the social life of human communities was almost entirely the expression of Folk Spirits (Archangels).[21] Their own soul, character or super-personality became (as it still does today in some communities) the culture or national character of the human community under its guidance. Social life in ancient times lacked any kind of personal freedom. The kings or tribal leaders directed the clan chieftains who in turn, directed the family head and so on down the social chain of command, the ultimate top-down leadership style. It was not so long ago that marriages were arranged by the family and even today in First World countries some parents still try to influence the future of their children from the model which they in turn received from their parents. As mentioned in the beginning of this essay, in some primitive communities that still exist in remote corners of the world, the power of the folk spirit is such that every aspect of life is determined and governed by strict tribal laws and codes of conduct.

In some indigenous communities or tribes, the ego presence is so faint, that the tribal Folk Spirits are even brought into partial incarnation. This can be seen in some initiatory dances, where after long and exhausting preparations inducing a state of trance, the dancers begin to move as one being. For those privileged to witness such events, they describe that at the moment of incarnation, of that moment when the individual dances become 'one being', a presence of immense power is felt. The participants in the dance were already collectively the folk soul of the Folk Spirit, and as we have seen in Rwanda, would willingly go to war sacrificing themselves for the tribe, now within the confines of the initiatory dance, they become the physical body of the folk spirit. For the witness, what was seen was much more than the sum total of the dancers, it was the tribal spirit itself. Each dancer became a limb of that being. Such tribal spirits or minor archangels are still dimly experienced in Europe and America where they are perceived in the different dialects in a nation's language. One marked trait of human beings who no longer stand beneath a tribal or Folk Spirit is that whatever language they speak as their mother tongue, they do so free of dialect. Such people stand rather under the Spirit of the Age. The recent trend in England to encourage the use of the dialects, particularly in broadcasting, could well be described as retrogressive.

Of all the world's nations Israel is arguably one of the most fervent in the pursuit of its mission in which religious and political traditions are merged within nationalism. The history of the Jews and their trials spanning nearly four thousand years against almost continual opposition can serve as a picture of the strength of a folk spirit in inspiring and nurturing its people. The Jews were led out of Egyptian slavery by Yahweh or Jehovah who, through Moses, determined every aspect of their lives. How they should live; what and how they should eat; what was considered a crime and what punishment that crime warranted. The Jews became free from the physical enslavement of the Egyptians but are still today enslaved to their Folk Spirit resulting in the ongoing crisis in the Middle East. Although the indications show that individuation in humankind is escalating, at least in the Western world, many millions still live under the domination of folk spirits or archangels.

Carl Gustav Jung's reference to a collective unconscious bears a greater reality when it can be seen to be much more than a description of a particular phenomenon, but the sentient body or folk soul of an archangel in its manifestation within a human community. In addition to archangelic inspiration we also now see the shadow manifestation of a group demon in which not inspiration takes place but group incitement. When human beings submerge their consciousness into a state of mass hysteria, whether that be in support of a football team, or some political or religious ideology, we see the working of destructive spiritual entities. Such entities — or rather we can justifiably call them demons — unleash unbelievable power for short periods of time and are behind the violence in riots and other destructive mob activity. Nurtured by hate, these group demons fade when individuals regain their consciousness.

As a human being develops through the stages of infancy, childhood, youth, maturity, old age and then death, so too do the Celestial Hierarchies go through through stages or cycles of growth in their working with humankind. Time Spirits of the age, and Folk Spirits of nations and peoples go through development and decay so that new impulses can enter into human development. Rudolf Steiner describes how when a Time or Folk Spirit remains active beyond its time or its mission, its soul begins to harden and decay directly affecting the culture or community under its sway. The moral and social collapse before its final dissolution, was the fate of the Roman and other similar empires.

Spiritual investigation by Rudolf Steiner has shown the enormous complexity of both the development and sadly, in some instances, the retrogression of the Celestial Powers in the development of the universe. In addition to the members of the nine hierarchies, other spiritual entities are continually being created out of, and by our human thinking, feelings and deeds, some out of good will and some out of enmity and hatred. These entities unconsciously created by us also strongly affect our lives and our communities on earth.[22]

Malignant beings from the ranks of the principalities and powers, as described by St.Paul, stand behind the rule of men like Hitler and Stalin, giving demonic support to the brutish control of people. The Bolsheviks came to power in Russia in 1917 with the support of only 2% of the total population. Prior to the revolution, Russia was the fastest growing economic and cultural power on earth.[23] Human evolution seems to proceed against tremendous forces of hindrance. On the one hand humankind is moving away from the domination or guidance of the folk spirits towards a global culture of freedom, whilst on the other, national, social, tribal, political and religious groupings are hardening into sclerotic forms inspired by retrogressive beings. Such beings have been described as working counter to the evolution of humankind and would bind humanity into a state of ego-less domination thereby denying the development of love into the world. Love can only blossom in freedom; the freer the individual, the greater the capacity for love.

With the appearance of the Christ into the physical world two thousand years ago in which the capacity of love brought to humanity by Gautama Buddha was given its content, a change in the relationship between human beings and the angelic world took place. This change took place through the kindling of love within the human ego itself through the sacrificial Deed of the Christ on Golgotha. This Christ-love became the substance and form of the human higher ego itself, thereby replacing in time the outer soul form enforced upon human groupings by the folk spirits or Archangels. Rudolf Steiner describes the Deed of the Cosmic Christ as the Turning Point of Time for human and earthly evolution. What was previously imposed upon mankind by benign Celestial Beings for mankind's advancement, could after the advent of Christ, only happen in freedom and love. Love, in care and responsibility for one's fellow human beings coupled with personal freedom are the hallmarks of future development. So far we have not seen much happening in the sphere of love and freedom, but two thousand years is only a brief whisper in cosmic time.

With the advent of the modern age it was possible for a truly global culture to form. For the past hundred years the cultural trend has been the gradual spread of Anglo-American or Western materialism world wide. Now each major city looks and feels just like the others: whether it be Sydney, Hong Kong, Hamburg or Los Angeles the gesture is the same, a general world culture in which building design is international (and mainly boring) and Coke is the drink, Calvin Klein is the gear, and English is the language. English in recent decades has become the world language for trade and technology. Even when a Japanese airliner approaches Tokyo airport, the exchange between the pilot and the control tower is conducted in English.

This development of a global culture has brought the possibility of freedom from the old folk souls and the traditions that kept a firm hold on peoples but it has also left us with a rather bland lifestyle of pop music, videos and parties, the sort of lifestyle portrayed in cigarette advertisements where young people are seen sporting in exotic places. In this culture, it seems that there is no place for anyone over the age of 35! The emphasis is on the here and now; the ambition is acquisition of either status or things or both with values that are based upon health, wealth and longevity. Until recently, spirituality has not been a consideration of this culture. Now with the ecological, social and economic chaos facing modern man, a new wave or paradigm which has broken through the barrier of materialism is beginning to show itself, a paradigm which may be the herald a new culture, a culture of caring. A culture of free individuals who voluntarily unite themselves into a world community no longer restrained by nationalism or racism, and where individuality is expressed through the free acceptance of responsibility for themselves and others out of true empathy. But every new culture has also its shadow. The coming culture will have its problems and challenges maybe even more dramatic and terrifying than those that face us now.

A possible preparation for this new culture could be seen in the new independent school movements like Freinet, Human Scale Education and in particular Rudolf Steiner's Waldorf Schools. In Steiner schools, children are recognised as having a spiritual heritage, and in which education assists them to meet and prepare for their personal destiny within the culture at large. Personal spiritual strivings may also have a greater recognition in the coming culture as they could be seen as enhancing the community as a whole. The rose that adorns herself, adorns the garden.

With the entering of the Christ into human evolution, and the great change in the relationship between humankind and the folk spirits, preceding divisions of humanity into races and nations may gradually

193

come to an end. All divisions except the moral one! It seem that the New Human is coming, but so also the New Beast-man.[24] All racial characteristics and regional differences may disappear as the New Human emerges together with the creation of a fifth kingdom on earth, a kingdom midway between the animals and humankind. With every step forward in development, a sacrifice is made and the kingdom of the New Brute will be the burden to be carried by the New Human.

It seems that our task in the near future is in the formation of a new community of peoples, no longer controlled from above, but out of the compassion of our own hearts, out of our own empathy and out of clarity of thought. In the past, peoples were led, not only by the folk spirit but by the ancestral spirits of their forefathers and linked by blood ties. In the coming culture, people will once again become aware of the participation of higher beings in the evolution of human-kind but they will no longer be united by blood but by common values and strivings accepted in freedom and love.

South Africa stands openly once more on the world stage as its people strive together to create a new community, a community in which all shall be free, and all shall be responsible. Our task is to help clear the dross from the stage upon which it will take place by assisting with the removal the dead thinking and meaningless tradi-tions that bind us to the past. By cultivating the ground from which it will spring. By developing an education based upon the under-standing of child development, and enacted as a truly caring vocation. By caring for the earth and its creatures as if we ourselves were their creators. We, as South Africans and as World Citizens have to choose: we can strive towards the creation of a new culture, or perish with the dying one — the decision is ours. The step in consciousness needed is enormous but when seen against the great descent into chaos that is now looming before us, it is quite small. All we need is courage, the same courage that gave the Europeans the strength to leave their homes and countries and travel to new shores and new lives. The courage that took the Vikings across the stormy oceans on their open boats, the courage that pitted young men against the charge of a raging lion alone as an initiation into manhood. Our age has made us complacent and soft, adventures are only to be read about, or seen on television, so we need extra strength but mainly we need courage, the courage to cross new thresholds into the uncharted realms of the spirit to take us onto the next step in our long journey through time on our way to becoming truly human.

BIBLIOGRAPHY

1. R. Steiner. *The Evolution of Consciousness.*
2. S. Covey, *The Seven Habits of Highly Effective People.*
3. F. Voigt, *Sects,Drugs and Rock n' Roll.*
4. E. Kant, *Critique of Pure Reason.*
5. R. Steiner, *Goethe the Scientist.*
6. A. Shepherd, *Scientist of the Invisible.*
7. E. Lehrs, *Man or Matter.*
8. W. Zeylmans van Emmichoven, *The Reality in Which we Live.* B. Lievegoed, *Man on the Threshold.*
9. R. Steiner, *Occult Science.*
10. *Ibid.*
11. *Ibid.*
12. B. Appleyard, *Understanding the Present.*
13. E. Lehrs, *Man or Matter.*
14. A. Bittleston, *Our Spiritual Companions.*
15. *Ibid.*
16. *Ibid.*
17. *Ibid.*
18. R. Steiner, *Mission of Folk Souls.*
19. St Paul, Epistle to the Ephesians 6:12.
20. *Ibid.*
21. R. Steiner, *Mission of Folk Souls.*
22. K. Markides, *The Magus of Strovolos.*
23. P. Johnson, *History of the World from 1917 to the 1980s.*
24. M. Scott Peck, *The People of the Lie.*

The Von Hardenberg Foundation

— *The Novalis Institute* —

The Von Hardenberg Foundation (which operates as The Novalis Institute) was established in Durban, South Africa, in 1982 as a vehicle for contributing to social and cultural change, by a group of people inspired by the Austrian scientist, educationist and spiritual researcher, Dr Rudolf Steiner. The Section 21 Company (Not For Gain) was registered and Novalis became a legal entity in 1984.

The founding group — Yvonne Oates (interior designer), Carol Ross (chartered accountant), Brian Johnson (architect) and Ralph Shepherd (businessman) — sought to offer their various professional talents in the development of innovative and creative processes for the educational, social and cultural problems of the day. This group was supported by many others including Stan Maher, now an active member of The Novalis Institute's management team. The founding group was based firmly upon the Systems or Holistic thinking[1] of

Rudolf Steiner. Over the years, Novalis staff have also been inspired by contemporary thinkers such as Fritjof Capra, Maurice Berman, Stephen Covey, Peter Senge, Vaclav Havel and South Africans Steve Biko and Adam Small, all of whom have striven to expose the inadequacies of the Cartesian or western materialistic view of the world.

Members of The Novalis Institute believe that social and cultural transformation from the current model based upon Western materialism to a more human-centred model must be preceded by individual change. Social change either in the individual or the community requires a paradigm shift in consciousness and not merely the adoption of another ideology, dogma or world view Å political, religious or philosophical. A total change in the way in which we see the world or in the way in which we think is required. Such transformation can only be experienced and described in retrospect. The process employed to initiate such a change is based upon personal introspection and contemplation in which personal and human values and principles are considered against the destructive effects of Western materialism. All those people mentioned above, in particular Rudolf Steiner, have written extensively about the exercises and processes involved in acquiring this change in consciousness.

Until recent years, such processes were considered to be the 'suspect' domain of (sometimes dubious) Eastern gurus and of New Age enthusiasts, and were not thought to be worthy of serious consideration. However, with the startling discoveries in atomic theory, which have stood a measurement-oriented physics on its head, together with the continuing collapse of the Darwinian theory of evolution for similarly compelling reasons, mankind is increasingly released from the thought prison of the Cartesian mindset in which the universe was seen as an immense machine, and all living things as chance chemical phenomena within a meaningless time/space continuum. In its place is the concept of an Intelligent and ordering universe to which human beings need to relate.

With this background the first Novalis team initiated a series of projects relating to cultural and social issues. However it soon became apparent that education would become the major focus of The Novalis

Institute's work. This meant the establishment of a teacher training programme in which educators would be introduced to a more holistic and effective philosophy and practice of education. Such an approach seeks to completely transform teachers' views of their vocation, the teaching being built around the needs of the child, instead of fitting pupils into an education factory system. Only an enlivened and human education can develop capacities and build the initiative and self-reliance which enable pupils to become initiative-takers and job creators, able to shape their own lives effectively and become producers as well as consumers. This would happen through the founding of a new college, for in the words of Albert Einstein, "The significant problems we face cannot be solved at the same level of thinking we were at when we created them"[2]. In a similar vein we cannot expect the social, cultural and economic problems of our time to be solved by thinking coming from the same institutions — universities or research institutes — who themselves have come into being out of the same thinking or paradigm that created these problems in the first place. Experience has shown that most established institutions can only consider "those innovations that might logically evolve out of the current system"[3] they seem incapable of considering a radical change in the system itself, that is, the possibility of operating under a different paradigm altogether. Hence the need for entirely new institutions that can operate out of new thinking, new paradigms, uncluttered by the past.

Since 1986 the main work of Novalis has developed in the Western Cape Province and KwaZulu/Natal regions in South Africa, the main office being situated in Cape Town, with a full-time staff of 14, supported by many part-time teacher trainers. In addition, Novalis can call upon support from professional consultants in the artistic, architectural and organisational development spheres who share and support the aims and objectives of The Novalis Institute.

The Novalis programmes have reached over 6000 state school teachers who were introduced to innovative primary and senior primary courses and the programmes have therefore impacted upon over 240 000 children. These programmes were designed to make education more meaningful for teachers and pupils and relevant to social and vocational needs. During recent years (1995/6) Novalis has been conducting democratisation and capacity building programmes based on the newly established Schools Bill of 1996 which provides for schools to become self-managing through democratically elected councils chosen from parents and teachers, and in the case of high schools, pupils as well. This step forward in development has left many schools and their communities in a state of bewilderment and even anxiety for they have had no previous background in such processes. Novalis facilitators have developed unique training programmes in consultation with the recipient communities covering issues of "Responsibility and Freedom," "Conflict Resolution," "Community Building," "Managing Change," "Democratisation," etc. Over 200 schools and communities have undergone training through The Novalis Institute. The potential for real community development through this programme in which the school is seen as the catalyst of change and true community building is enormous. Novalis is currently conducting teacher enrichment programmes in Zimbabwe at the request of state and private school teachers. Similar requests led Novalis' Eddie Dawes to visit Kenya and Tanzania where plans are being made to send teachers to Cape Town for shorter or longer periods of training.

The highlight in the history of Novalis is its move into its own building, the Novalis Ubuntu Centre for Continuing Education. Designed by the staff together with Novalis Board Member and architect Brian Johnson (current President of the South African Institute of Architects and Deputy President of the Africa Institute of Architects), the building is organically and ecologically designed on the basis of Human Scale architecture and is funded by private individuals, corporate donors and international funding agencies. The building houses the training programme for in-service teachers and governance programmes for schools as well as a home base for the teacher outreach programme. Its unusual forms and curved dome attracts many visitors and well-wishers.

The Novalis Press now has six titles in print, this book being one of them. All of them have been produced as text books for the various programmes being conducted. Sales of these books to outside agencies help in a small way as revenue generation for the running costs of the Institute. Novalis is supported by grants, donations and bequests, without which it could not, at this stage, continue with its work in disadvantaged communities.

REFERENCES

1 Also called Goetheanistic thinking after Wolfgang von Goethe, who, together with Frederich von Hardenberg (Novalis) and William Blake, stood in opposition to the materialistic philosophy of Descartes, the science of Newton and the economics of Malthus.

2 *The Seven Habits of Highly Effective People*, p 42, by Stephen Covey. Simon & Schuster 1994.

3 *The Different Drum*, p 8, by M. Scott Peck. Rider, 1990.

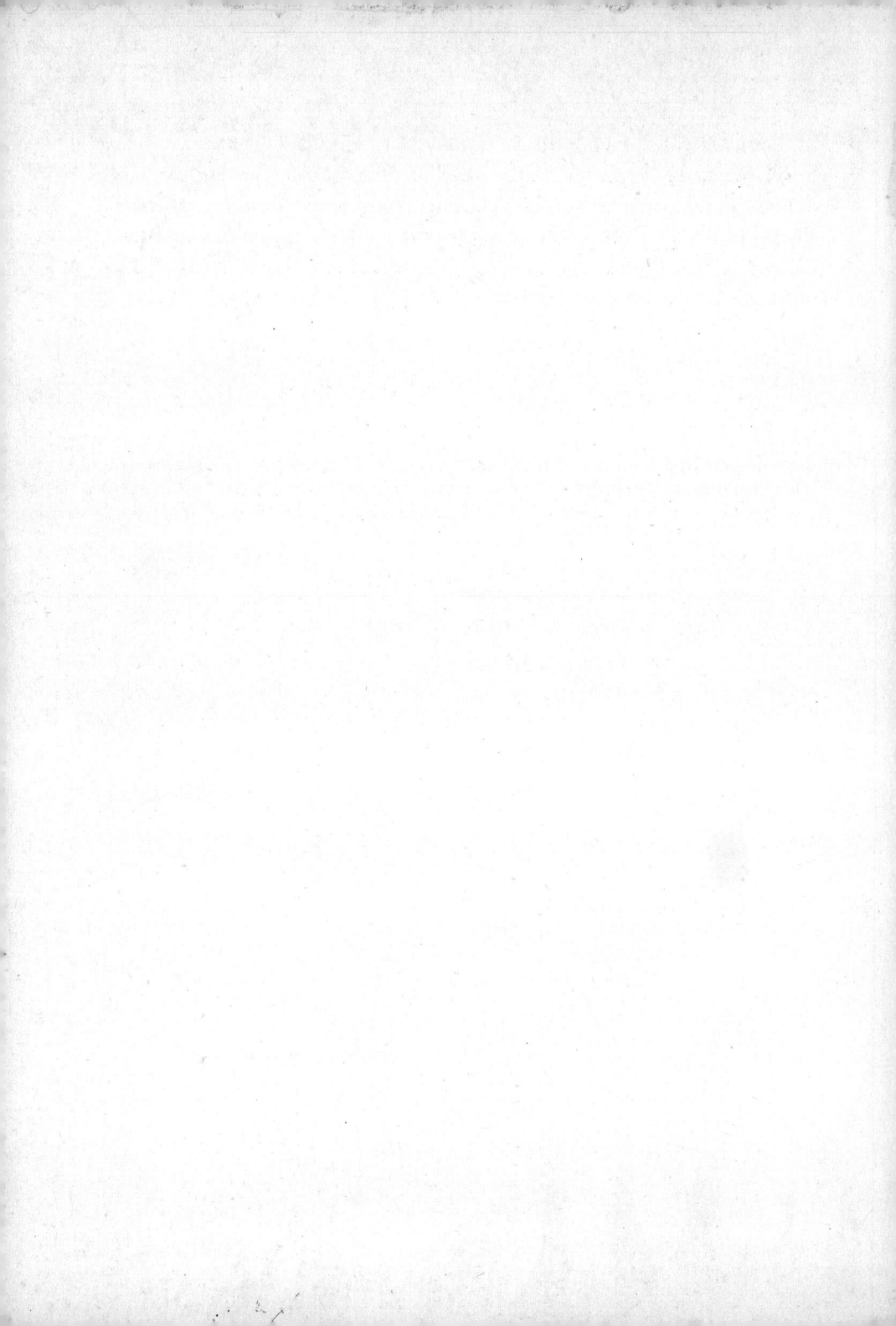